THE ENVIRONMENT

THE ENVIRONMENT

Other Books of Related Interest

THE
ENVIRONMENT

Laura K. Egendorf, *Book Editor*

Bruce Glassman, *Vice President*
Bonnie Szumski, *Publisher*
Helen Cothran, *Managing Editor*

OPPOSING
VIEWPOINTS®
SERIES

GREENHAVEN PRESS
An imprint of Thomson Gale, a part of The Thomson Corporation

THOMSON
™
GALE

Detroit • New York • San Francisco • San Diego • New Haven, Conn.
Waterville, Maine • London • Munich

333.7
E

LIBRARY OF CONGRESS CATALOGING-IN-PUBLICATION DATA

The environment : opposing viewpoints / Laura K. Egendorf, book editor.
  p. cm. — (Opposing viewpoints series)
Includes bibliographical references and index.
ISBN 0-7377-2230-4 (lib. : alk. paper) — ISBN 0-7377-2231-2 (pbk. : alk. paper)
  1. Environmental degradation. 2. Environmental protection. 3. Nature—Effect of human beings on. 4. Environmental policy. I. Egendorf, Laura K., 1973– .
GE140.E533 2005
333.7—dc22   2004049292

Printed in the United States of America

"Congress shall make no law...abridging the freedom of speech, or of the press."

First Amendment to the U.S. Constitution

The basic foundation of our democracy is the First Amendment guarantee of freedom of expression. The Opposing Viewpoints Series is dedicated to the concept of this basic freedom and the idea that it is more important to practice it than to enshrine it.

Contents

Why Consider Opposing Viewpoints?

"The only way in which a human being can make some approach to knowing the whole of a subject is by hearing what can be said about it by persons of every variety of opinion and studying all modes in which it can be looked at by every character of mind. No wise man ever acquired his wisdom in any mode but this."

John Stuart Mill

In our media-intensive culture it is not difficult to find differing opinions. Thousands of newspapers and magazines and dozens of radio and television talk shows resound with differing points of view. The difficulty lies in deciding which opinion to agree with and which "experts" seem the most credible. The more inundated we become with differing opinions and claims, the more essential it is to hone critical reading and thinking skills to evaluate these ideas. Opposing Viewpoints books address this problem directly by presenting stimulating debates that can be used to enhance and teach these skills. The varied opinions contained in each book examine many different aspects of a single issue. While examining these conveniently edited opposing views, readers can develop critical thinking skills such as the ability to compare and contrast authors' credibility, facts, argumentation styles, use of persuasive techniques, and other stylistic tools. In short, the Opposing Viewpoints Series is an ideal way to attain the higher-level thinking and reading skills so essential in a culture of diverse and contradictory opinions.

In addition to providing a tool for critical thinking, Opposing Viewpoints books challenge readers to question their own strongly held opinions and assumptions. Most people form their opinions on the basis of upbringing, peer pressure, and personal, cultural, or professional bias. By reading carefully balanced opposing views, readers must directly confront new ideas as well as the opinions of those with whom they disagree. This is not to simplistically argue that everyone who reads opposing views will—or should—change his or her opinion. Instead, the series enhances readers' understanding of their own views by encouraging confrontation with opposing ideas. Careful examination of others' views can lead to the readers' understanding of the logical inconsistencies in their own opinions, perspective on why they hold an opinion, and the consideration of the possibility that their opinion requires further evaluation.

Evaluating Other Opinions

To ensure that this type of examination occurs, Opposing Viewpoints books present all types of opinions. Prominent spokespeople on different sides of each issue as well as well-known professionals from many disciplines challenge the reader. An additional goal of the series is to provide a forum for other, less known, or even unpopular viewpoints. The opinion of an ordinary person who has had to make the decision to cut off life support from a terminally ill relative, for example, may be just as valuable and provide just as much insight as a medical ethicist's professional opinion. The editors have two additional purposes in including these less known views. One, the editors encourage readers to respect others' opinions—even when not enhanced by professional credibility. It is only by reading or listening to and objectively evaluating others' ideas that one can determine whether they are worthy of consideration. Two, the inclusion of such viewpoints encourages the important critical thinking skill of objectively evaluating an author's credentials and bias. This evaluation will illuminate an author's reasons for taking a particular stance on an issue and will aid in readers' evaluation of the author's ideas.

It is our hope that these books will give readers a deeper understanding of the issues debated and an appreciation of the complexity of even seemingly simple issues when good and honest people disagree. This awareness is particularly important in a democratic society such as ours in which people enter into public debate to determine the common good. Those with whom one disagrees should not be regarded as enemies but rather as people whose views deserve careful examination and may shed light on one's own.

Thomas Jefferson once said that "difference of opinion leads to inquiry, and inquiry to truth." Jefferson, a broadly educated man, argued that "if a nation expects to be ignorant and free . . . it expects what never was and never will be." As individuals and as a nation, it is imperative that we consider the opinions of others and examine them with skill and discernment. The Opposing Viewpoints Series is intended to help readers achieve this goal.

David L. Bender and Bruno Leone,
Founders

Greenhaven Press anthologies primarily consist of previously published material taken from a variety of sources, including periodicals, books, scholarly journals, newspapers, government documents, and position papers from private and public organizations. These original sources are often edited for length and to ensure their accessibility for a young adult audience. The anthology editors also change the original titles of these works in order to clearly present the main thesis of each viewpoint and to explicitly indicate the opinion presented in the viewpoint. These alterations are made in consideration of both the reading and comprehension levels of a young adult audience. Every effort is made to ensure that Greenhaven Press accurately reflects the original intent of the authors included in this anthology.

Introduction

"Society has an obligation to reduce the environmental burdens [minority and poor] communities disproportionately experience."
—*Center for Progressive Regulation*

"Genuine environmental justice reform must focus on both environmental protection and preserving economic stability."
—*David W. Almasi,* executive director of the National Center for Public Policy Research

In Roxbury, a Boston neighborhood with a largely minority population, 19 out of every 1,000 children under the age of four has been hospitalized because of asthma. By comparison, Massachusetts's overall asthma rate is 3.6 children per 1,000, or one-fifth that of Roxbury. This discrepancy is one of many pointed to by some environmentalists, who decry what they see as "environmental injustice"—the fact that neighborhoods populated by poor people and minorities are more likely to be situated near toxic waste dumps, sewage treatment facilities, and polluting factories. The location of these neighborhoods means that their residents may be more vulnerable to asthma and other diseases. Environmental justice has now become one of the most debated issues concerning the environment. Since the 1970s, environmentalists and the federal government have led efforts to create a more environmentally just nation. However, these efforts have been criticized by those who argue that in their fervor to make poorer neighborhoods more environmentally safe, these environmentalists and politicians are preventing job growth.

The environmental justice movement began in the late 1970s, following the revelation that a working-class neighborhood in Niagara Falls, New York, had been built near the Love Canal toxic waste dump. Understandably fearful after discovering that eighty-eight toxic chemicals had migrated into surrounding areas from the dump, the residents demanded that the state assist in relocating them. After the state government refused, community members protested. These protests resulted in President Jimmy Carter ordering an evacuation, with the federal and state governments funding the relocation. The Love Canal incident led in 1980 to Congress's passage of the Superfund Act, which gave the federal government increased control over the release of hazardous substances into the environment, obligated polluters to pay for contaminating the land, and created a tax on the petroleum and chemical industries. The cleanup of abandoned hazardous waste sites is funded through revenues from that tax. As of 2004, 263 sites have been cleaned up and another 583 sites have been decontaminated.

Superfund has not been the only way in which the federal government has aided the cause of environmental justice. In 1992 William Reilly, the head of the Environmental Protection Agency (EPA) during George H.W. Bush's administration, established the Office of Environmental Justice in order to address concerns of environmental justice advocates. Two years later, President Bill Clinton issued Executive Order 12898, which required the EPA to include environmental justice in its policies. However, Superfund and the EPA have not completely erased environmental injustice. A 1987 study by the Commission for Racial Justice for the United Church of Christ found that minority communities are three times likelier than whites to be located near commercial waste, treatment, storage, and disposal facilities. The Center for Progressive Regulation, a research and educational organization which supports regulations that protect the environment, also contends that the EPA is not completely color-blind. According to the center,

> The divestment and blight that accompanies areas with more than their share of contaminated sites leaves people of color and poor persons who live nearby in a difficult situation. The first problem is that these areas have to compete with other contaminated sites for government cleanup resources. [A] 1992 *National Law Journal* report, . . . supports the claims of environmental justice advocates that sites in their communities are often neglected or receive less effective cleanups than sites in wealthier, predominantly white areas.

Making neighborhoods cleaner and promoting environmental justice might seem admirable, but critics of the environmental justice movement caution that placing too much emphasis on ridding poorer areas of factories and waste sites can have negative economic consequences. In his report, *The Time Is Now for a New Environmental Justice Policy*, Michael J. Centrone, a research associate at the National Center for Public Policy Research, a research foundation that supports free-market solutions to environmental challenges, writes that EPA policies prevented a steel company from building a mill that would have created two hundred jobs in an impoverished Michigan community. Centrone and other critics of environmental justice policies assert that many environmental justice groups also question the emphasis of EPA regulations. For example, thirty-nine of the sixty-nine environmental justice organizations surveyed by the National Center stated that a balance needed to be established between environmental goals and economic opportunities. Jonathan Adler of the Heartland Institute, a research foundation that promotes market-based solutions to environmental protection, encapsulates this view when he writes, "By erecting the greatest barriers to economic development in those communities with disproportionate minority populations, 'environmental justice' has a disparate impact on the people it purports to help."

Protecting poor and minority populations from environmental injustice while not denying them economic opportunities presents a complex challenge to activists. Indeed, most of the world's environmental problems have provoked intense debate as those concerned struggle to devise solutions. In *Opposing Viewpoints: The Environment*, the authors examine the condition of the environment and possible solutions to environmental problems in the following chapters: Is There an Environmental Crisis? How Can Pollution Best Be Prevented? Is the American Lifestyle Bad for the Environment? What Policies Will Improve the Environment? A world without any ecological troubles is unlikely to ever exist, but the solutions offered in this book might go a long way toward mitigating some of the most thorny environmental problems facing the world today.

CHAPTER 1

Is There an Environmental Crisis?

Chapter Preface

Each year as many as fifty thousand animals and plants become extinct, while hundreds more become endangered. While some of these species are exotic creatures that have little impact on the lives of most people, animals that provide protein to more than 1 billion humans each day—fish—are also at risk. According to journalist Colin Woodard, author of *Ocean's End: Travels Through Endangered Seas*, approximately 120 of the major commercial fish species are in decline or completely exploited. What causes the loss of swordfish, sea bass, and other fish is highly controversial.

In the view of many environmentalists, the fishing industry is to blame for the decreasing fish supply. Environmentalists argue that fishermen catch more fish than necessary to meet demand. Woodard asserts that improved technology, such as radars and satellite navigation, have made it easier to locate—and therefore decimate—fish. He places particular blame on industrial-scale fishing operations, describing them as "too large, effective, and wasteful for nature to support." He and others critical of the industry note that by being so effective, these operations create two problems. First, as popular species begin to run out, fishermen begin catching less-desired, smaller fish in order to remain economically viable; however, these smaller fish are the food supply for the more popular fish, which makes it harder for those endangered species to make a comeback. Second, the trawls and nets used to catch fish often fatally snare other species not eaten by humans, including dolphins and sea turtles.

The fishing industry, however, asserts that environmental degradation, in particular water pollution and the loss of coral reefs, is the reason for vanishing species. As Mary H. Cooper, a writer who specializes in environmental issues, explains, "[Non-point pollution is] the runoff of fertilizers, pesticides, oil residue and other contaminants from cultivated fields, lawns and streets. Nitrogen and phosphorous in fertilizers reduce oxygen levels in the water, smothering fish and the underwater grasses they need to survive, while encouraging toxic blooms of algae that kill even more fish." The fishing industry points out that coral reefs are also being destroyed because of pollution and warming reef waters. As the reefs die, so do the fish and other creatures that live around them. Since 70 percent of the reefs in existence today may be gone by 2050, countless fish may also be at risk.

A number of responses have been suggested to thwart the loss of fish, including shutting down industrial-scale fishing companies, establishing marine reserves, and giving more power to local fishermen, who are more likely to protect fish that are important to their communities' regular diet. Unless one or more of these solutions is effective, the world could lose more than one hundred important fish species. The issue of endangered species is just one of many purported environmental woes. The authors in this chapter debate other global environmental problems. With the world more interconnected now than in centuries past, the state of the global environment is more important than ever.

"The world is moving into uncharted territory as human demands override the sustainable yield of natural systems."

An Environmental Crisis Exists

Lester Brown

In the following viewpoint Lester Brown asserts that the environment is deteriorating as humanity's demands on the earth's resources increase. According to Brown, two of the most serious ecological problems are rising temperatures, caused by the burning of fossil fuels, and falling water tables. He contends that these troubling conditions have made it more difficult for farmers to produce enough food to feed the world's people. Brown concludes that the damaging trends that began during the twentieth century must be reversed, lest the world experience social and economic collapse. Brown is the founder and chairman of the Worldwatch Institute, an independent research organization whose goal is the creation of an environmentally sustainable society.

As you read, consider the following questions:
1. According to the team of scientists discussed by Brown, when was the earth's regenerative capacity first surpassed?
2. How do higher temperatures lead to lower crop yields, as explained by Brown?
3. According to the author, what are "environmental refugees"?

As world population has doubled and as the global economy has expanded sevenfold over the last half-century, our claims on the earth have become excessive. We are asking more of the earth than it can give on an ongoing basis, creating a bubble economy.

We are cutting trees faster than they can regenerate, overgrazing rangelands and converting them into deserts, overpumping aquifers, and draining rivers dry. On our cropland, soil erosion exceeds new soil formation, slowly depriving the soil of its inherent fertility. We are taking fish from the ocean faster than they can reproduce.

We are releasing carbon dioxide (CO_2) into the atmosphere faster than nature can absorb it, creating a greenhouse effect. As atmospheric CO_2 levels rise, so does the earth's temperature. Habitat destruction and climate change are destroying plant and animal species far faster than new species can evolve, launching the first mass extinction since the one that eradicated the dinosaurs 65 million years ago.

Consuming the Earth

Throughout history, humans have lived on the earth's sustainable yield—the interest from its natural endowment. But now we are consuming the endowment itself. In ecology, as in economics, we can consume principal along with interest in the short run, but in the long run it leads to bankruptcy.

In 2002, a team of scientists led by Mathis Wackernagel, an analyst at Redefining Progress, concluded that humanity's collective demands first surpassed the earth's regenerative capacity around 1980. Their study, published by the U.S. National Academy of Sciences, estimated that our demands in 1999 exceeded that capacity by 20 percent. We are satisfying our excessive demands by consuming the earth's natural assets, in effect creating a global bubble economy. . . .

The Effects of Population and Income

Humanity's demands on the earth have multiplied over the last half-century as our numbers have increased and our incomes have risen. World population grew from 2.5 billion in 1950 to 6.1 billion in 2000. The growth during those 50 years exceeded that during the 4 million years since we emerged as a distinct species.

Incomes have risen even faster than population. Income per person worldwide nearly tripled from 1950 to 2000. Growth in population and the rise in incomes together expanded global economic output from just under $7 trillion (in 2001 dollars) of goods and services in 1950 to $46 trillion in 2000, a gain of nearly sevenfold.

Population growth and rising incomes together have tripled world grain demand over the last half-century, pushing it from 640 million tons in 1950 to 1,855 million tons in 2000. To satisfy this swelling demand, farmers have plowed land that was highly erodible—land that was too dry or too steeply sloping to sustain cultivation. Each year billions of tons of topsoil are being blown away in dust storms or washed away in rainstorms, leaving farmers to try to feed some 70 million additional people, but with less topsoil than the year before.

Demand for water also tripled as agricultural, industrial, and residential uses climbed, outstripping the sustainable supply in many countries. As a result, water tables are falling and wells are going dry. Rivers are also being drained dry, to the detriment of wildlife and ecosystems.

Fossil fuel use quadrupled, setting in motion a rise in carbon emissions that is overwhelming nature's capacity to fix carbon dioxide. As a result of this carbon-fixing deficit, atmospheric CO_2 concentrations climbed from 316 parts per million (ppm) in 1959, when official measurement began, to 369 ppm in 2000. . . .

Agricultural Challenges

As we exceed the earth's natural capacities, we create new problems. For example, farmers are now facing two new challenges: rising temperatures and falling water tables. Farmers currently on the land may face higher temperatures than any generation since agriculture began 11,000 years ago. They are also the first to face widespread aquifer depletion and the resulting loss of irrigation water.

The global average temperature has risen in each of the last three decades. The 16 warmest years since recordkeeping began in 1880 have all occurred since 1980. With the three warmest years on record—1998, 2001, and 2002—coming in the last five years, crops are facing heat stresses that are without precedent.

Water's Role in the Environment

About 250 million hectares are irrigated worldwide today, nearly five times more than at the beginning of the twentieth century. Irrigation has helped boost agricultural yields and outputs and stabilize food production and prices. But growth in population and income will only increase the demand for irrigation water to meet food production requirements. Although the achievements of irrigation have been impressive, in many regions poor irrigation management has markedly lowered groundwater tables, damaged soils, and reduced water quality.

Water is also essential for drinking and household uses and for industrial production. Access to safe drinking water and sanitation is critical to maintain health, particularly for children. But more than 1 billion people across the globe lack enough safe water to meet minimum levels of health and income. Although the domestic and industrial sectors use far less water than agriculture, the growth in water consumption in these sectors has been rapid. Water is integrally linked to the health of the environment. Water is vital to the survival of ecosystems and the plants and animals that live in them, and in turn ecosystems help to regulate the quantity and quality of water. Wetlands retain water during high rainfall, release it during dry periods, and purify it of many contaminants. Forests reduce erosion and sedimentation of rivers and recharge groundwater. The importance of reserving water for environmental purposes has only recently been recognized.

Mark W. Rosegrant, Ximing Cai, and Sarah A. Cline, *Environment*, September 2003.

Higher temperatures reduce crop yields through their effect on photosynthesis, moisture balance, and fertilization. As the temperature rises above 34 degrees Celsius (94 degrees Fahrenheit), photosynthesis slows, dropping to zero for many crops when it reaches 37 degrees Celsius (100 degrees Fahrenheit). When temperatures in the U.S. Corn Belt are 37 degrees or higher, corn plants suffer from thermal shock and dehydration. They are in effect on sick leave.

Each such day shrinks the harvest.

In addition to decreasing photosynthesis and dehydrating plants, high temperatures also impede the fertilization needed for seed formation. Researchers at the International Rice Research Institute in the Philippines and at the U.S. Department of Agriculture have together developed a rule of thumb that each 1-degree-Celsius rise in temperature above the optimum during the growing season reduces grain yields by 10 percent.

These recent research findings indicate that if the temperature rises to the lower end of the range projected by the Intergovernmental Panel on Climate Change, grain harvests in tropical regions could be reduced by an average of 5 percent by 2020 and 11 percent by 2050. At the upper end of the range, harvests could drop 11 percent by 2020 and 46 percent by 2050. Avoiding these declines will be difficult unless scientists can develop crop strains that are not vulnerable to thermal stress.

Water Tables Are Falling

The second challenge facing farmers, falling water tables, is also recent. With traditional animal- or human-powered water-lifting devices it was almost impossible historically to deplete aquifers. With the worldwide spread of powerful diesel and electric pumps during the last half-century, however, overpumping has become commonplace.

As the world demand for water has climbed, water tables have fallen in scores of countries, including China, India, and the United States, which together produce nearly half of the world's grain. Water tables are falling throughout the northern half of China. As the water table falls, springs and rivers go dry, lakes disappear, and wells dry up. Northern China is literally drying out. Water tables under the North China Plain, which accounts for a fourth or more of China's grain harvest, are falling at an accelerating rate.

In India, water tables are also falling. As India's farmers try to feed an additional 16 million people each year, nearly the population equivalent of another Australia, they are pumping more and more water. This is dropping water tables in states that together contain a majority of India's 1 billion people.

In the United States, the third major grain producer, water tables are falling under the southern Great Plains and in California, the country's fruit and vegetable basket. As California's population expands from 26 million to a projected 40 million by 2030, expanding urban water demands will siphon water from agriculture.

Scores of other countries are also overpumping their aquifers, setting the stage for dramatic future cutbacks in water supplies. The more populous among these are Pakistan, Iran, and Mexico. Overpumping creates an illusion of food security that is dangerously deceptive because it enables farmers to support a growing population with a practice that virtually ensures a future drop in food production.

A Steep Rise in Water Demand

The water demand growth curve over the last half-century looks like the population growth curve, except that it climbs more steeply. While world population growth was doubling, the use of water was tripling. Once the growing demand for water rises above the sustainable yield of an aquifer, the gap between the two widens further each year. As this happens, the water table starts to fall. The first year after the sustainable yield is surpassed, the water table falls very little, with the drop often being scarcely perceptible. Each year thereafter, however, the annual drop is larger than the year before.

In addition to falling exponentially, water tables are also falling simultaneously in many countries. This means that cutbacks in grain harvests will occur in many countries at more or less the same time. And they will occur at a time when the world's population is growing by more than 70 million a year.

These, then, are the two new challenges facing the world's farmers: rising temperatures and falling water tables. Either one by itself could make it difficult to keep up with the growth in demand. The two together provide an early test of whether our modern civilization can cope with the forces that threaten to undermine it. . . .

Reversing Dangerous Trends

Unless we quickly reverse the damaging trends that we have set in motion, they will generate vast numbers of environmental refugees—people abandoning depleted aquifers and exhausted soils and those fleeing advancing deserts and rising seas. In a world where civilization is being squeezed between expanding deserts from the interior of continents and rising seas on the periphery, refugees are likely to number not in the millions but in the tens of millions. Already we see refugees from drifting sand in Nigeria, Iran, and China.

We are now looking at the potential wholesale evacuation of cities as aquifers are depleted and wells go dry. Sana'a, the capital of Yemen, and Quetta, the capital of Pakistan's Baluchistan province, may become the early ghost towns of the twenty-first century.

A reversal of the basic trends of social progress of the last half-century has long seemed unthinkable. Progress appeared inevitable. But now we are seeing reversals. As noted earlier, the number of hungry may be increasing for the first time since the war-torn decade of the 1940s. And a rise in life expectancy—a seminal measure of economic and social progress—has been interrupted in sub-Saharan Africa as a result of the HIV epidemic. As millions of able-bodied adults die, families are often left with no one to work in the fields. The disease and spreading hunger are both weakening immune systems and reinforcing each other, something epidemiologists had not reckoned on.

Uncharted Territory

The failure of governments to deal with falling water tables and the depletion of aquifers in the Indian subcontinent could be as disruptive for the 1.3 billion living there as the HIV epidemic is for the people in sub-Saharan Africa. With business as usual, life expectancy could soon begin to fall in India and Pakistan as water shortages translate into food shortages, deepening hunger among the poor.

The world is moving into uncharted territory as human demands override the sustainable yield of natural systems. The risk is that people will lose confidence in the capacity of their governments to cope with such problems, leading to social breakdown. The shift to anarchy is already evident in countries such as Somalia, Afghanistan, and the Democratic Republic of the Congo.

Business as usual—Plan A—is clearly not working. The stakes are high, and time is not on our side. . . . The good news . . . is that there are solutions to the problems we are facing. The bad news is that if we continue to rely on timid, incremental responses, our bubble economy will continue to grow until eventually it bursts.

*"The wilderness was saved by . . .
technologies and fuels."*

An Environmental Crisis Does Not Exist

Peter W. Huber

The environment, particularly that of the United States, is thriving, Peter W. Huber contends in the following viewpoint. According to Huber, an environmental rebirth began in the 1920s, which can largely be credited to the impact of technology. He claims that through the use of pesticides, fossil fuels, and preservatives, among other scientific advances, Americans are able to make more efficient use of their land. Therefore, Huber maintains, more land is allowed to remain wilderness. Huber is a senior fellow at the Manhattan Institute's Center for Legal Policy, an organization that researches public policy issues.

As you read, consider the following questions:
1. How has America's economy been transformed since 1920, in Huber's view?
2. According to the author, why are poorer nations unsuccessful at conservation?
3. In Huber's opinion, what is the preoccupation of modern environmentalists?

Peter W. Huber, "No, the Sky Is NOT Falling," *Hoover Digest*, Winter 2001.

B eginning about 1920 and continuing to this day, we have witnessed . . . a magnificent environmental renaissance—the massive reforestation of the Adirondacks and much of America's northeastern forests. And with the return of the forests has come the return of bears, cougars, and moose.

What happened? Did we simply shift our logging to the forests of the Pacific Northwest? Some of it, yes. But the numbers for the country as a whole are very heartening, too. Since about 1920, the United States has returned a huge amount of land to forest—somewhere between 20 and 140 million acres. For purposes of comparison, all our cities, roads, suburbs, all the places where we actually live and work and drive, occupy about 60 million acres. For the last 80 years or so, now, our human footprint on the continent—the amount of wilderness we directly displace with our cities, farms, and coal mines—has been steadily shrinking.

A Reversal of Trends

This represents a fundamental reversal of trends that prevailed for the prior three centuries. From the time of the Pilgrims until 1920, our human footprint on the continent steadily expanded while the forests and the wilderness steadily retreated. And then, some time around 1920, we reversed course.

The story—at least in my telling of it—gets even better. The prevailing winds blow west to east across North America. Today, on the continent itself, we burn enough fossil fuel to release some 1.6 billion metric tons of carbon into the air each year. Yet—as best we can measure these things directly—carbon dioxide levels drop as you move across the continent. They are *lower* in the mid-Atlantic than in the mid-Pacific.

So—to put the question again—what happened? Let me frame the answer as provocatively as possible: the wilderness was saved by the technologies and fuels that the modern green establishment is doing its utmost to tax, curtail, and ultimately abolish.

It comes down to this: what has changed since 1920 is that we transformed our economy from 40 acres and a mule to 4 acres and a fossil fuel. We moved from energy and construction materials derived from wood to modern counterparts extracted from deep in the earth. We moved from two-dimensional technologies that spread humanity out across the *surface*, across the wilderness, to three-dimensional technologies with which we extract most of our materials, energy, and wealth from the sterile depths. The most important single component of the change? We stopped growing our energy and instead learned to dig most of it out of the ground.

Today, our main remaining use of the surface is agriculture. We use six acres of farm and eight of range for every one acre of city, suburb, and highway. But those acres have been shrinking dramatically too—we cultivate about the same total amount of land as we did 100 years ago, even as we produce four times as much food. How?

Fossil fuels made possible rapid, long-distance transportation. This let us move our farms from comparatively bad soil and climate—near to where we live—to good soil and climate at a much greater distance. Our farmers didn't trade one acre of Adirondacks for one acre of prairie, they traded five for one. For the wilderness as a whole, that was a very good trade.

Per-acre yields have also been substantially increased by the intelligent use of artificial fertilizers and pesticides. There may be some adverse effects, but the raw numbers are beyond serious dispute. And there's an excellent chance, again, that for the wilderness as a whole the overall exchange was very favorable indeed.

The Importance of Pesticides

To illustrate the positive impact of technology on the environment, consider this example: T.R. [President Theodore Roosevelt] gives a speech in 1905, explaining to Americans that they need to conserve national forests to ensure adequate supplies of wood for the future building of railroads. That same year, however, railroad companies begin coating their ties with creosote, stopping the termites. The chemical preservative triples the ties' lifespans, which effectively slashes the demand for wood in that context by two-thirds. In the decades since, wood preservatives and termite eradication have done far more to save forests in America than, say, the recycling of newspapers.

We could trace a whole raft of comparable environmental impacts from pesticides, preservatives, food irradiation, plastic packaging, and (most recently) genetic engineering. They can all have comparable effects: they sharply reduce losses along the food chain, from farmer's field to dining room table, with commensurate reductions in agricultural sprawl. When horses and grasshoppers eat less of our food, we use fewer acres to grow it.

A Positive Future

The great movie producer Sam Goldwyn used to say, "Never prophesy—especially about the future." It is unavoidable, however, in the case of the environment, because the environment is all about the future. There is every reason to think that our grandchildren will drive emission-free autos and will routinely say, "Smog—what was *that* all about?" Notwithstanding the puzzling problems of climate change and habitat loss, the likelihood is that in 100 or 200 years, our successors will enjoy a thriving environment.

Steven Hayward, *World & I*, March 2002.

None of this means we should use pesticides recklessly. It does mean that we have to think very hard about acres and how they get saved—or risk condemning the very technologies most instrumental in saving them. And at the end of day, there can be little serious doubt that many of the technologies that the modern green establishment criticizes most vehemently have in fact been critically important in saving the wilderness and reforesting the continent.

Once one grasps what has been happening to land use and forest cover on the continent, it is much less surprising to come across direct measurements that suggest that North America is *sinking* more carbon than it emits. It's not too hard to guess where all that carbon is going—into new trees, new underbrush, new soil, and new carbon-rich landfill. It is going back into the earth. One soda can's worth of carbon, back into every square yard of surface, every year. Enough, apparently, to sink back into the ground all the carbon we mine and drill out of it.

Can carbon sinking continue forever? Of course not. Nothing continues forever. But the massive deforestation brought about by our grandparents and great-grandparents has left enormous amounts of room for reforesting. Another doubling and redoubling of our agricultural productivity—readily imaginable with the power of genetic engineering now at hand—could free up a great deal more space for forest and wilderness. In the Third World, which is still deforesting, the opportunities are even larger. Simply halt the deforestation, and we'd cut greenhouse emissions by almost 30 percent. Reverse it—begin reforesting—and for a good long time you can stop net greenhouse emissions completely.

The Wealth-Growth Paradox

Until quite recently, humanity's advance meant retreat for the wilderness. The surface—land, river, and shallow coastal waters—supplied all our food, building materials, and fuel. The more we grew, the more land we seized. And the more the wilderness retreated.

For much of this century, however, that process has been reversed. That is the fundamental paradox of growth and wealth. With the past century's hard technologies, economic growth has not ended up consuming more land, it has ended up consuming *less*. If all wealth came from the surface, this would have been impossible: expanding the economy would inevitably mean shrinking the wilderness. But wealth doesn't have to come from the surface, and for most of this century, it hasn't—not in America. Hard technology has severed the link between wealth and land. Poorer countries, by contrast, remain horrible at conservation because they don't have, and can't afford, the technology that has allowed us to escape our dependence on the surface.

Something even more profound went wrong with the population models we set before T.R. in 1901. We don't have 600 million people in the United States. And we aren't likely to, unless they arrive from other countries. Putting aside the effects of immigration—a zero-sum game—the total fertility rate (roughly, the average number of children born per woman, per lifetime) in more developed regions (like ours) has fallen to 1.6 today—almost 25 percent below the replacement rate.

The direction of things is now the same in developing

countries as they grow wealthier. The fertility rate in India today is lower than the American rate in the 1950s. Fertility rates in most sub-Saharan African nations are falling steadily. If the trajectories of rising global affluence and failing fertility stay on their present courses, world population—about 6 billion today—will peak at about 10 billion in 2050, then will start shrinking.

Wealth, in short, seems to be very effective in curtailing fecundity. Nobody knows exactly why, but the correlation is much too strong to question. The poor reproduce as [economist Thomas] Malthus said they would—as fast as they can—and pay a fearful price in the high mortality and dismal prospects of their offspring. They are "inefficient" here, if such a cold-hearted word can be used to describe child mortality. The rich secure their genetic posterity through quality, not quantity.

Wealth, then, is the best answer to the sprawl of the human genome. Green is what people become when they feel personally secure, when their own appetites have been satisfied, when they do not fear for the future or for their own survival or their children's. It is wealth that gives ordinary families the confidence to be generous to the world beyond. It is the rich who can afford poverty, so to speak. It is they who can declare enough, enough, I need no more; it is now time for me to grow things other than myself. It is the rich who can be thin because they know they will always have plenty to eat. It is the rich who can cherish the wilderness because they no longer have to choose between their own survival and nature's.

Teddy Roosevelt's Legacy

That was certainly T.R.'s view of things. He was a wonderfully intuitive and spontaneous politician, of course, but his environmentalism was clearly anchored in an abiding (if patrician) love for unspoiled nature. He loved hunting, loved the outdoors. He recognized that private ownership wasn't conserving the wilderness spaces he cherished. So he set about addressing the problem with boundless enthusiasm and energy. And the fact is, a hundred years later, the conservation movement probably owes more to this maverick

Republican than to any other president before or since.

T.R.'s "environmentalism" was mainly about land, wilderness, and the great outdoors. The modern green establishment, in contrast, is preoccupied with microscopic and long-term, diffuse effects on large populations and their quantification by means of large computer models. It is T.R.'s political legacy that conservatives should be reclaiming today, for purely practical political reasons, to begin with. The wilderness-centered environmentalism that T.R. stood for is more popular than ever, especially in the politically critical West.

But conservatives can get beyond that kind of cynical calculation and should. The logic for a government role in wilderness conservation is easy to square with a political perspective that strongly favors free market forces in other arenas. Private conservation is important. But at some point the vastness of the Adirondacks, the Everglades, of river archipelagos and coral reefs—the sheer scope and scale of the most ambitious conservation objectives—requires a reach to match.

More fundamentally, wilderness is perhaps the most unusual "good" one can imagine in economic discourse: wilderness is, by definition, what's out there before the economists arrive, before the property lines are drawn and the fences erected. Markets can't produce what we value because it's not packaged, traded, bought, or sold, because it's spontaneous, open, and free.

This is also one area where conservatives can allay some of our deepest fears about the ineptitude of "big government." The central objective of wilderness conservation, after all, is to ensure that in some places, nothing much is done at all. *Nothing* is the one thing that big government is capable of doing quite well. Even conservatives can believe in government's ability to do that. T.R. certainly did.

Finally, conservatives can perhaps comfortably affirm that a place like Yellowstone National Park helps define what it is to be an American citizen. I'm quite sure that by any standard ecological metric that naturalists might come up with, Disney could run Yellowstone better than the National Park Service does. I suppose Disney could give us a better flag and a better national anthem, too. But still, it wouldn't be the same, and I think conservatives should be comfortable saying that.

But the question then arises: How much political space do such views then leave between the new T.R. (whoever he may turn out to be) and, say, the old Al Gore? The answer, as I have attempted to show, is quite a bit. There remain strong, indeed fundamental, differences about how concrete, practical policies and technologies are likely to advance the kind of environmentalism that T.R.—equipped only with a monocle, not a Power-Mac—so clearly understood and so passionately embraced.

"As the warming proceeds, there is only a greater tendency to disrupt climates globally."

Global Warming Is a Serious Problem

George M. Woodwell

In the following viewpoint George M. Woodwell maintains that global warming is a potentially devastating environmental problem that must not be ignored. He asserts that global warming, which numerous scientists and environmentalists believe is caused by the burning of oil, coal, and gas, can lead to changes in weather patterns, a sharp rise in the sea level, and the spread of tropical diseases. According to Woodwell, the United States must take a leadership role to help restore climatic stability. Woodwell is the founder and director of the Woods Hole Research Center, which uses education and scientific research to address climate change, global warming, and other environmental issues.

As you read, consider the following questions:
1. According to the author, what made monitoring of the atmosphere possible?
2. How many tons of carbons are released each year because of the destruction of forests, as stated by Woodwell?
3. How does Woodwell compare climatic disruption and slavery?

George M. Woodwell, "Fiddling While the World Burns," *Amicus Journal*, (www.nrdc.org/onearth), vol. 23, Spring 2001, pp. 31–32. Copyright © 2001 by George M. Woodwell. Reproduced by permission.

S ix billion people have filled the world to overflowing and feel so good about it that they promise to add two billion more in just a decade or two. There are a few problems: space to live, water to drink, air to breathe, a global disruption of climate, and a progressive loss of the benefits of civilization over large sections of the earth.

In regions where wealth has accumulated, these global exigencies seem remote. But the big issues of governance have to do increasingly with environment, and those issues do not go away. The overriding one is the global disruption of climate.

Decades of Evidence

The problem is not new. It was recognized and defined more than a century ago by scientists who realized even then that burning coal and oil and gas would increase the amount of carbon dioxide in the atmosphere and warm the earth. Accurate measurements of the composition of the atmosphere, however, had to wait until infrared gas analysis was invented. Instruments became available in the 1950s that could, for all practical purposes, detect a single molecule of carbon dioxide in the atmosphere. These instruments made it possible to monitor the atmosphere around the world.

Suddenly, data were available showing a year-by-year accumulation of carbon dioxide in the atmosphere. They showed, also, powerful evidence of the importance of the interactions between the atmosphere and natural ecosystems: an annual cycle of rising and falling carbon dioxide concentrations following the seasonal metabolism of northern-hemisphere forests. In data collected in the 1960s at Brookhaven National Laboratory's meteorology tower, my colleagues and I could see the carbon dioxide concentration in the atmosphere fall every summer as the forests of North America took up carbon, and rise every winter as respiration dominated over photosynthesis and the forests released carbon. It was clear that forests have a very large role in determining the composition of the atmosphere. Such a thought was heresy at the time, but is now universally accepted.

The scientific community, taken as a whole, is conservative. Yet it has been forthright and surprisingly effective in defining the problem of global climatic disruption and its urgency. That definition has accumulated over a full century, but the work has been especially rapid and urgent since 1970, when preparations were underway for the 1972 international Stockholm Conference on the Human Environment.

At that time there were data showing the changes in the composition of the atmosphere but no data showing any consequences, and the scientific community was restrained in its comments. But for scientists to refrain from voicing the logical prediction that the accumulation of heat-trapping gases would warm the earth was a denial of their own experience and knowledge; to refrain from urging that steps be taken to avoid that disruption was a denial of the very utility of science. Over the decade, the community came to accept its appropriate role. Scientists increasingly began voicing warnings. Hearings were held in Congress. Steps were taken to strengthen subsidies for alternatives to fossil fuels. Solar panels for hot water were installed on the White House as an example for the nation.

Action Has Not Been Taken

Under the Reagan administration, however, those initiatives were canceled. The solar panels were removed, with the purpose of setting a different kind of example. Two decades of delay ensued, punctuated by only halting progress and virtually no leadership from government in resolving a clear threat to the public welfare.

[More] recently, the Sixth Meeting of the Parties to the Framework Convention on Climate Change, held in November [2000] in The Hague, failed. The nations were neither imaginative enough nor flexible enough to reach agreement on implementing the Kyoto Protocol's provisions for reducing carbon emissions. The meetings need not have failed had the United States offered the enthusiastic and constructive leadership that the world expects and depends on. Instead, the Clinton administration approached the talks with a retrograde bargaining position, in deference to a recalcitrant U.S. Congress.

The [George W. Bush] administration, drawn heavily from the wealth of the oil patch and allied interests, seems certain to delay constructive action still further. The world at the moment is at an impasse. Every day that passes is another delay won by the petroleum and other fossil fuel interests and their allies.

The impasse cannot be allowed to continue. Time is short. The problem does not offer the world decades to dither. The price of inaction mounts daily and raises the potential for massively costly environmental surprises, beyond any modern experience or capacity for correction.

The Effects of Carbon Dioxide

The carbon dioxide content of the atmosphere is 33 percent higher now than it was in the latter part of the nineteenth century and rising daily. The total release of carbon from burning coal and oil and gas is now about 6.5 billion tons annually. There is an additional release of carbon from the destruction of forests, about 1.6 billion tons annually. Of that sum 3 to 4 billion tons accumulate every year in the atmosphere. There they cause the rapid, continuous warming of the earth as a whole; changes in precipitation patterns; migration of climatic zones at a rate of one to several kilometers per year; the melting of glaciers; an accelerated rise in sea level; an expansion of the regions affected by the great tropical diseases; and an increased range and frequency of climatic extremes, including large storms. These changes are not hypothetical. They are measurable now and accelerating.

Where does the rest of the carbon dioxide go, the difference between the total emitted and the accumulation in the atmosphere? It is absorbed by diffusion into the surface layer of the oceans; apparently, it is also absorbed into forests of the northern hemisphere that are expanding into lands abandoned from agriculture in the late nineteenth and early twentieth centuries. As the earth warms most of these "sinks" for carbon dioxide are diminished. Other sources of carbon, such as the decay of organic matter in soils and in the peat of the tundra, appear. So there is no cure for the warming in the warming itself. As the warming proceeds, there is only a greater tendency to disrupt climates globally. No end is in sight on the present course until the world exhausts its supplies of coal and oil and gas sometime in the next few centuries.

Meanwhile, the heat-trapping gases continue to accumulate in an atmosphere that has already accumulated enough potential for further warming, unrealized as yet but awaiting us in the future, to take the world far beyond the range of reliable predictions. If by some magic we were to realize immediately and fully the objective of the Framework Convention on Climate Change—stabilization of the heat-trapping gas content of the atmosphere at the current level—this further warming would still occur over years to come. It will push the climate well beyond the realm of what scientists can predict in any detail and into the realm of surprises.

Troubling Implications

Just what are the implications, for example, of an Arctic Ocean that is consistently open in summer, no longer a cold, reflective white surface of ice but a warm, black surface of open water, free to absorb the heat of the twenty-four-hour summer sun through evaporation? The global climate is driven by the latent energy of water vapor; what will be the effects of a large new source of this energy entering at the polar extreme? At what point in the disruption of the global climatic system will the circulation of the oceans suddenly shift, altering the flow of the Gulf Stream, which now carries heat to northern Europe and keeps coasts ice-free in the north as far east as Novaya Zemlya? What are the costs around a world of 6 billion people when continental centers become progressively arid and increasingly subject to extremes of climatic variation?

Further, what are the implications of the progressive impoverishment of forests and other stable landscapes as chronic changes in climate become acute? The biophysical stability of the human habitat is totally dependent on the stability of the functions of natural ecosystems. Destabilization moves the world down the slippery slope of biotic impoverishment. To see the result in its extreme form, we need look only to Haiti, where the landscape and concomitantly the people have become so thoroughly impoverished that no government can stand long enough to establish a program of recovery.

Responding to Global Warming

What is to be done? We hold the chart and the possibility of rescue. What is needed now is U.S. leadership, strong and effective leadership in realizing the full objectives of the Framework Convention on Climate Change, which we and 180 other nations have ratified and made the law of the whole earth. The first step is for the United States to develop its own plan for encouraging first the conservation of fossil fuels and then their displacement as the main source of energy driving industrial society. A host of studies show economic advantages as well as environmental stability emerging from this transition. . . .

Wasserman. © 2000 by *The Boston Globe*. All rights reserved. Reproduced by permission of Tribune Media Services.

The issue is a global emergency, a disaster underway. It is not a potential threat. It is with us now and gathering costs, immediate and future, daily. If we can maintain a $300-billion-a-year military establishment against potential threats of potential enemies, if we can cruise around the world underwater with enough nuclear weapons to turn the world to a cinder in a few hours with no earthly enemy in sight, we can marshal tens of billions to the purpose of restoring climatic stability to the only human habitat.

Perhaps the worst example in U.S. history of a ruinous policy left standing, long past the time it had been recognized as a destructive curse, is slavery. Climatic disruption and slavery are in no way similar problems; nor does the moral position of those who use fossil fuels begin to approach that of one who lays claim to owning a human being. But in each case, the policymakers who colluded through inaction in the perpetuation of the problem did so with full knowledge of the scale of the evil. In the case of slavery, political expediency, seen always as necessity, was allowed to dictate a compromise and enabled the drafters of the Constitution to remain silent on a practice grossly inconsistent with the principles of the Declaration of Independence and the dreams for the new nation. The ultimate price was greater than even the most vigorous, shrill, and imaginative abolitionists anticipated: more than 75 further years of slavery, followed by 600,000 deaths in a bitter civil war whose scars remain, 140 years later, and are made the deeper by festering problems with race.

In the case of climate, expediency is again turning a blind eye to a destructive curse. Once again, those who make the choice—the wealthy of the United States, the worst carbon culprits, who share the greatest capacity for instituting the needed changes—will suffer least. Once again, others—such as the many poor of the world who will drown or starve in Bangladesh, sub-Saharan Africa, and the Pacific Islands—will pay the highest price. The costs of our scandalous neglect are with us now, accumulating daily, and they will be levied on all the world's billions, here now and to come.

*"The promoters of global warming ignore
repeatedly occurring cold spells."*

Global Warming Is Not a
Serious Problem

John F. McManus

Numerous scientists have refuted the notion of global warming, John F. McManus asserts in the following viewpoint. According to McManus, these scientists contend that while the
amount of carbon dioxide in the atmosphere has increased,
the gas does not affect the world's climate and is in fact beneficial to the environment. McManus concludes that any
changes in climate, whether heat waves or cold spells, occur
naturally and that global warming extremists are simply using
scare tactics in order to control the behavior of their fellow
citizens. McManus is the publisher of *New American* and the
president of the John Birch Society, an organization that supports personal freedom and limited government.

As you read, consider the following questions:
1. According to studies by a Canadian geologist and Israeli
   astrophysicist, what is the chief cause behind the rise of
   atmospheric carbon dioxide?
2. How many people died in a cold wave that hit India in
   2002, according to McManus?
3. In the author's opinion what is an indication of the
   "moral bankruptcy" of global warming enthusiasts?

John F. McManus, "The Sky Is Falling! Or Is It?" *New American*, vol. 19,
September 8, 2003, pp. 9–13. Copyright © 2003 by American Opinion
Publishing Incorporated. Reproduced by permission.

The steady stream of scary scenarios about global warming and its supposed cataclysmic consequences hasn't abated. It continues because its purveyors have an agenda that encompasses much more than environmental concerns. Those who insist that human beings, especially Americans, are endangering the future of mankind by causing the Earth's atmospheric temperature to rise ignore the many scientific refutations of their claims. What they seek is control of fellow man: how he lives, how he works, and whether constitutional limitations on his government shall endure. In their drive for power, they are regularly aided by elements of the Establishment media that also ignore sound science.

One significant example of the ongoing fright peddling is when Senators John McCain (R-Ariz.) and Joseph Lieberman (D-Conn.) managed to obtain a commitment from the full Senate that it will, before the year [2003] ends, consider their proposal to mandate controls on industrial emissions of carbon dioxide (CO_2).[1] The two senators insist that atmospheric CO_2 must be reduced because it is the main cause of global warming. Predictably, Senator McCain argued that a voluntary approach to this problem wasn't acceptable because it did not "meet the urgency" of the threat.

Almost simultaneously, the governors of 10 northeastern states announced plans to spend the next two years developing a regional strategy to limit carbon emissions at coal- and oil-fired power plants in their areas. Their motive stemmed from the supposed need to combat global warming, a condition they too claim results from CO_2 being pumped into the atmosphere by man's burning of fossil fuels.

Applauding both of these developments, the *New York Times* editorialized that a great deal more must be done "to slow the warming trend" that is an "issue of great public concern on which the world has spoken clearly."

Debunking the Global Warming Scare

If leading politicians and the nation's leading newspaper agree that global warming is a serious problem, who dares to disagree? The answer is that a lengthening list of highly

---

1. The measure failed by a 55-43 vote.

trained meteorologists, climatologists, geophysicists, and others in related scientific fields have, for decades, insisted that the political and journalistic doomsayers are wrong and that there is no global warming problem. These individuals continue to issue a stream of scientifically based responses that debunk the CO_2 and global warming scares. We present only some of their findings by posing questions of our own and letting trained experts supply answers. In some cases, we shall cite the absurdities supplied by the non-scientific doomsayers.

Question: *Has any senator risen to combat the McCain/Lieberman proposal?*

Answer: On July 28th, Senator James Inhofe (R-Okla.), chairman of the Senate's Committee on Environment and Public Works, delivered an important speech attacking the claims of global warming alarmists and others who issue warnings about similarly unproved environmental threats. Senator Inhofe cited an array of scientific authorities to debunk the claims of "environmental extremists." He closed his remarks by urging colleagues to reject measures designed to treat nonexistent problems because they are "designed not to solve an environmental problem, but to satisfy the ever-growing demand of environmental groups for money and power. . . ."

What about the House of Representatives? Have its members been provided sound scientific perspective about carbon dioxide emissions and global warming?

On May 28, 2003, Dr. John R. Christy testified before the Committee on Resources of the U.S. House of Representatives. A professor of Atmospheric Science and director of the Earth System Science Center at the University of Alabama at Huntsville, Dr. Christy pointed out that carbon dioxide "is not a pollutant" and that its beneficial effect on plant life "is the lifeblood of the planet." Specifically addressing claims that CO_2 is causing planetary warming, Dr. Christy added: "Climate models suggest that the answer is yes; real data suggest otherwise." He is only one of a growing number to point to inaccuracies stemming from reliance on climate models intended to predict the weather many years in the future.

Addressing widespread insistence that man's activity has caused recent warm weather, Dr. Christy, the recipient of awards from both NASA and the American Meteorological Society, pointed to several studies indicating that "the climate we see today is not unusual at all." He noted that, in 2000, "the U.S. experienced the coldest combined November and December" in over 100 years and that "the 19 hottest summers in the past century occurred prior to 1955." He assured the House Committee members, "looking at these events does not prove the country is experiencing global cooling any more than a hot July represents global warming."

Why Carbon Dioxide Levels Are Rising

Does man's burning of fossil fuels actually account for most of the increased amount of CO_2 in the atmosphere?

The July issue of the Geological Society of America's *GSA Today* presented the results of independent studies conducted by a Canadian geologist and an Israeli astrophysicist. The two scientists agree that atmospheric CO_2 is rising, but they contend that interplay between solar activity and cosmic rays from deep space, not man's activity, is the chief cause of this increase. Jan Veizer of the University of Ottawa and Nir Shaviv of Hebrew University of Jerusalem had arrived at this conclusion independently of each other. The two met [in October 2002] when they discovered their findings to be astoundingly similar. Their conclusions square with the claims of internationally renowned scientists Sallie Baliunas and Willie Soon, who have maintained for years that solar activity is the principal cause of climate fluctuations.

Is more CO_2 in the atmosphere actually a good development?

If healthy plant life is desirable, more CO_2 should be a goal because plants consume CO_2 just as animals (including humans) consume oxygen. Dr. Robert Balling, the director of climatology at Arizona State University, claims that increased CO_2, far from being harmful, is extremely beneficial. Referring to literature presented in publications produced for botanical scientists, Dr. Balling notes that there are "thousands of articles showing that elevated concentrations of CO_2 will be beneficial for plants." Dr. Balling cited experiments where plants grown with elevated levels of CO_2

were compared to similar plants grown without increasing the concentration of the supposedly dreaded gas. From New Zealand to America, the results reported in major peer-reviewed scientific journals are the same: Plants grown in the presence of additional CO_2 showed greater growth, less need for water, greater drought tolerance, and increased ability to deal with plant stresses. Instead of viewing CO_2 as a degrading pollutant, Dr. Balling urges fellow Americans to "drive out to the forest and feel good about the CO_2 coming out of your tailpipe!"

Global Warming May Be Beneficial

Almost all climate models predict that global increases in temperature will be greater toward the North and South Poles, and locations close to the equator will experience less —and possibly little—warming. In other words, temperatures in Miami a hundred years from now may be about what they are today, but Minneapolis temperatures on average may be considerably warmer. Climate models also predict that the greatest warming impacts will be in the winter and at night, just the times when a little more warmth might be most appreciated in places like Minneapolis.

It is beginning to sound as though global warming is an answer to someone's prayers. Instead of complaining, maybe we should be thanking our lucky stars. Canada and Siberia may boom. Indeed, Yale University economist Robert Mendelsohn writes, in a study published by the American Enterprise Institute, that there has been a "near revolution" during the past five years in predictions of the socioeconomic impacts of global warming. It now appears that "many countries will benefit from warming. . . . The industrialized nations of the earth happen to lie in boreal and temperate climates, where warming is likely to prove beneficial."

Robert H. Nelson, *Liberty*, February 2003.

Didn't world leaders agree at 1997's UN-sponsored conference held in Kyoto, Japan, that industrialized nations must reduce CO_2 emissions to combat global warming?

Yes, delegates from many nations accepted the Kyoto Protocol, which would, according to the U.S. Energy Information Administration, cost the United States as much as $283 billion annually. But, as Cato Institute's Mario Lewis states, adopting the Kyoto guidelines "would have almost no effect on global temperatures." Basing his conclusions on the work of such eminent scientists as Massachusetts Institute of Technology's Dr. Richard Lindzen, Lewis maintains that forecasts of greater warming of the planet "are based on questionable climate history, implausible emission scenarios, and unconfirmed feedback effects." He urges Congress to reject "the flawed science and exaggerated claims of those who predict catastrophic global warming." Yet the House International Relations Committee recently approved a "Sense of the Congress" resolution introduced by Rep. Bob Menendez (D-N.J.) that advocates Kyoto-style suppression of domestic industrial activity to prevent impending climate catastrophe.

Recent identical headlines in the New York Times *and* Los Angeles Times *claimed that "Arctic Ice Is Melting at Record Level." Doesn't this indicate global warming?*

Researchers from the Norwegian Polar Institute and the Norwegian Meteorological Institute have compiled data from ships' logs dating back five centuries. These entries show that the current "retreat of ice observed in the Arctic occurred previously, in the early 1700s." In an article appearing in the *Toronto Globe and Mail*, Chad Dick of the Arctic Climate Systems Study pointed to "natural cycles in sea ice extent" and stated that low levels of ice 300 years ago occurred before there were any significant man-made emissions of greenhouse gases such as CO_2. Also, the American Geophysical Union's *EOS* magazine published an article by Igor Polyakov who examined Arctic ice and temperature records from 1868 onward and found no evidence to back up those sensational claims.

Similarly, the January 2002 issue of *Science* magazine published the findings of scientists who, after measuring Antarctic ice formations, concluded that the ice near the South Pole is growing thicker. Another article appearing in *Nature* magazine pointed to the research led by scientist Peter Doran, who discovered temperatures in the Antarctic to have decreased, not increased, over the past 30 years. These scientific findings are among many that prompt Professor Patrick Michaels of the University of Virginia's Department of Environmental Sciences to chastise the "liberal media" for badly misleading the public on global warming.

The Beginning of the Global Warming Scare

How did the claims about global warming arise?

Dr. James Hansen of the National Aeronautics and Space Administration is reputed to be the godfather of the global warming scare. From his prominent position at NASA, he claimed in 1988 to be "99 percent sure" that man's activity was responsible for causing a rise in the Earth's temperature. But, by 1999, he backed off from his dire assessment and stated: "The forces that drive long-term climate change are not known with an accuracy sufficient to define future climate change." Yet advocates of larger and more intrusive government continue to present global warming as a threat and man's supposed role in causing it as a fact.

Reports coming out of Europe in mid-2003 pointed to a deadly heat wave. Isn't this an indication that global warming is a fact?

The summer heat wave throughout much of Europe was indeed severe, with France's Health Ministry reporting on August 14th [2003] that the heat wave killed as many as 3,000 people in France. But only seven months earlier, in January 2003, Europe experienced unusually cold weather. During this unusually cold period, a rare snowfall hit central London and more snow surprised southern France. Germany and central Europe were also hard hit with freezing temperatures, snow drifts, and transportation blockages.

In December 2002, a separate cold wave in northern India claimed the lives of 1,500 persons and won designation as one of the top five global catastrophes of 2002. Only a few years earlier, in November 1998, an Arctic cold wave swept into Europe and claimed scores of lives.

The promoters of global warming ignore repeatedly occurring cold spells. But competent scientists don't ignore them; they contend that sharp fluctuations in weather conditions, producing either hot or cold, occur because of nature and are to be expected.

Have responsible scientists ever organized to challenge the claims about global warming and CO_2 emissions?

In 1998, a petition signed by more than 18,000 scientists sought to debunk the claims of global warming enthusiasts and even pointedly challenged the recommendations contained in the Kyoto Protocol. A letter from Dr. Frederick

Seitz endorsing its content and an eight-page article reviewing the available research literature on the topic accompanied the widely circulated petition. When pressed, Dr. Seitz, a past president of the National Academy of Sciences, refused to remove his endorsement of the project. The accompanying article, written by physical chemist Dr. Arthur Robinson, stated that "predictions of harmful climatic effects due to future increases in minor greenhouse gases like carbon dioxide are in error and do not conform to current experimental knowledge."

The petition, signed by thousands of meteorologists, climatologists and atmospheric scientists, stated in part: "There is no convincing evidence that human release of carbon dioxide, methane, or other greenhouse gases is causing or will, in the foreseeable future, cause catastrophic heating of the Earth's atmosphere and disruption of the Earth's climate."

Catastrophic Claims

In a world plagued with terrorism and other crises, just how serious is the global warming problem supposed to be according to the environmentalists?

In July 2003, England's John Houghton, a former co-chairman of the highly politicized United Nations Intergovernmental Panel on Climate Change, said that he "had no hesitation" in describing global warming as "a weapon of mass destruction." Adding to his hyperbole, Houghton stated, "Like terrorism, this weapon knows no boundaries [and] can strike anywhere in any form—a heat wave in one place, a drought or a flood or a storm surge in another." According to this once-respected former chief of the British Meteorological Office, global warming "kills more people than terrorism."

Have any claimants about the danger of catastrophic global warming expressed any doubts about their theory?

Dr. Stephen Schneider of the National Center for Atmospheric Research was quoted by the October 1989 issue of *Discover* magazine as saying that scientists are "ethically bound . . . to tell the truth, the whole truth, and nothing but. . . ." So far, so good. Yet, after claiming that the Earth faces "potentially disastrous climate change," he called on fellow global warming enthusiasts to "offer up scary scenarios, make simplified, dramatic statements, and make little mention of any doubts we might have." Compounding his willingness to deceive the public, he even suggested that colleagues had the option of choosing "between being effective and being honest."

What do these environmental extremists offer in place of the use of fossil fuels?

The "alternatives" usually advanced include solar, wind, and geothermal power. But the minuscule amounts of energy available from these alternative sources will never come close to matching the energy produced by coal, oil, and natural gas, the targeted fossil fuels. Indicative of the blindness and/or moral bankruptcy of most global warming enthusiasts is their almost universally negative attitude about safe, clean and efficient nuclear power.

[In the summer of 2003,] however, a group of MIT and Harvard scientists released a two-year study that boldly recommended increasing the number of America's nuclear power plants from 100 to 300. This is good news, even though the group accepts the false notion that carbon dioxide is "a greenhouse gas that contributes significantly to global warming."

What are the true goals of extreme environmentalists?

In 1972, Worldwatch Institute leader Lester Brown wrote that "an environmentally sustainable future requires nothing short of a revolution [that would include] restructuring the global economy, dramatically changing human reproductive behavior and altering values and lifestyles." In 1991, Canadian billionaire Maurice Strong, poised to serve as the Secretary-General of the 1992 UN Earth Summit held in Rio de Janeiro, wrote: "It is clear that current lifestyles and consumption patterns of the affluent middle class . . . involving high meat intake, consumption of large amounts of frozen and 'convenience' foods, ownership of motor vehicles, numerous electric household appliances, home and workplace air conditioning . . . suburban housing . . . are not sustainable."

In his 1992 book *Earth in the Balance*, then-senator Al Gore insisted that "the effort to save the global environment" must become "the central organizing principle for every institution in society." He called for a "wrenching transformation" of society that must include "completely eliminating the internal combustion engine" because it is "the single greatest threat to our civilization." Not surprisingly, he never gave up using his own automobiles, each of which possesses one of those supposed threats to civilization under its hood.

In 1993, the UN released *Agenda 21: The Earth Summit Strategy to Save the Planet*. This massive blueprint for regimenting "every person on Earth" calls for "a profound re-orientation of all human society." It calls for monitoring and controlling "the environmental consequences of every human action."

Many other examples could be cited showing that the real agenda behind the global-warming scare is about enchaining the planet, not saving it.

> *"The world's population is six billion and growing, and concern about population growth endures."*

Population Growth Causes Environmental Problems

John Attarian

One of the world's most influential economists was Thomas Malthus, who in 1789 wrote an essay in which he argued that the earth, being defined by limits, would not be able to provide sufficient resources for an unlimited number of people. In the following viewpoint John Attarian argues that while both sides of the population debate have misinterpreted Malthus, the economist has been proven correct. Attarian opines that environmental problems such as famines and water shortages indicate that the earth will not be able to sustain the world's growing population. Attarian is a freelance writer and frequent contributor to *World & I*.

As you read, consider the following questions:
1. What did William and Paul Haddock predict would happen to the world's food supply, as stated by the author?
2. According to Thomas Malthus, what are the three checks on population growth?
3. In Attarian's opinion, what was Malthus's essential argument?

In discussions of population, one almost invariably encounters the name Malthus. Thomas Robert Malthus, it is said, was a gloomy English economist who argued two centuries ago that population increases exponentially (doubling in every time period: 1, 2, 4, 8, . . .), whereas food supply increases arithmetically (by increments equal to the initial amount: 1, 2, 3, 4, . . .). According to this view, population will eventually outrun sustenance, so famine will inevitably wipe out the excess population. Supposedly history has exploded Malthus, because he failed to anticipate modern agriculture.

Yet like a perennial flower, Malthus keeps coming up. Both sides in the overpopulation debate use him as a polemical point of departure for their arguments. Thus a 1994 *Washington Post* article [by Jessica Matthews] titled "Malthus's Warning" pointed out that "so far, food supplies have not, as he predicted, been overtaken by human numbers"—then warned that we cannot be "confident that Malthus was wrong in more than his timing." Hunger and fatal malnutrition remain widespread, food production has been raised about as much as possible, and soil degradation is rising, so more funding for research on agricultural improvements is urgently needed. Five years later, another piece [by Nicholas Wade], "Why Malthus Was Mistaken," retorted that "Malthus's prediction that population growth is bound to outrun food production, condemning societies to perpetual misery and starvation, is much more than plain wrong." Not only is a geometric population growth rate, "assumed by Malthus to be the case at all times," not obtaining but food production is not stagnating.

The world's population is six billion and growing, and concern about population growth endures. The issues Malthus raised, then, are still alive. This suggests that a fresh look at his ideas is timely. How accurate is the mainstream depiction of Malthus? What did he really say? Is his theory really dead? What, if anything, does he still have to tell us?

The Popular Version of Malthus

Both sides of the population debate have invoked Malthus for decades. During the 1960s and '70s, a rash of books announced that explosive population growth would soon overwhelm Earth's ability to feed humanity and that disaster was imminent. In 1967 William Paddock, an agronomist, and Paul Paddock, a retired foreign service officer, argued that in the less developed countries (LDCs), population explosion would soon collide with stagnant food production. "The famines are inevitable," they warned. "Malthus, the economist, summarized it as graphically as is possible: population will increase in geometrical progression . . . but food will increase in arithmetical progression." Predicting famine by 1975, the Paddocks argued that America's food surplus wouldn't suffice to help all the LDCs, and that it should therefore be allocated according to "triage": deciding which countries did not need aid, which were beyond help, and which could be saved (and therefore should receive aid). . . .

Counterattacking, population optimists depicted the same Malthus but with a different message. In *The Ultimate Resource*, Julian Simon claimed that Malthus posited "constant geometric growth" in population, thus the core of his theory is that "population increases faster than does the means of sustenance and continues until the standard of living has fallen to bare subsistence." Malthus' theory claims, Simon wrote, that since fertility rises with income, the rising population consumes the rising income, so "there is a tendency for mankind to be squeezed down to a long–run equilibrium of living at bare subsistence." Dismissing this as simplistic, Simon retorted that "contrary to Malthus, constant geometric growth does not characterize the human population.". . .

Such is the general depiction of Malthus. It turns out that this is a serious misrepresentation.

Malthus' Writings

To grasp the real significance of Malthus' principle of population, knowledge of its context is essential. Thomas Robert Malthus (1766–1834) was ordained to the Anglican priesthood in 1788 after a thorough education including a solid grounding in mathematics. The French Revolution started the following year. Caught up in the enthusiasm surrounding the revolution, some intellectuals believed that humanity was both perfectible and on the verge of attaining an ideal society. The marquis de Condorcet, a moderate French revolutionary, argued in his *Esquisse d'un tableau historique des progres de l'esprit humain*[1] that progress unfolded naturally in a series of ten stages, the ninth one ending with the founding of the French Republic, the tenth and last being a world of abundance, harmony, and equality of wealth, gender, and opportunity. Similarly, William Godwin, father-in-law of the poet [Percy Bysshe] Shelley, foresaw a society of equality, peace, brotherhood, happiness, and altruism. Malthus' father had expounded earlier versions of these ideas eagerly to his son. Although kindly and sympathetic to social improvement, Malthus deemed these claims untenable and decided to debunk them.

Accordingly, in 1798 he wrote *An Essay on the Principle of Population*. It began with two postulates, which he saw as "fixed laws of our nature," namely that food is necessary for survival and that "the passion between the sexes" is necessary and will persist undiminished. The core of his principle of population followed: "Assuming then my postulata as granted, I say, that the power of population is indefinitely greater than the power in the earth to produce subsistence for man."

"Population, when unchecked, increases in a geometrical [exponential] ratio. Subsistence increases only in an arithmetical ratio. A slight acquaintance with numbers will shew the immensity of the first power in comparison with the second."

"By that law of our nature which makes food necessary to the life of man, the effects of these two unequal powers must be kept equal." "This implies a strong and constantly operating check on population from the difficulty of subsistence."

The inequality between the powers of population and subsistence and the need to equalize them, he added, "form the great difficulty that to me appears to be insurmountable" for attaining a perfect society.

Checks on Population Growth

Note the qualifier regarding geometric population growth: "if unchecked." Obviously, geometric growth refers to a theoretical situation, not an actual one. Based on the early experience of the United States, which was reality's closest ap-

1. *Sketch for a Historical Picture of the Progress of the Human Mind*

proach to an ideal situation of unconstrained population growth under favorable circumstances, Malthus argued that if unchecked, population could double every twenty-five years. He added, however, that "in no state that we have yet known" has population grown with "perfect freedom." Repeatedly, Malthus referred to the "constant operation of the strong law of necessity" restraining population growth, the "constant check upon population."

Two kinds of checks always operated, Malthus argued: preventive checks, which prevent population growth (such as deferring or forgoing marriage out of awareness of the difficulties of raising a family in poverty), and positive checks (for example, war, famine, pestilence), which remove existing people. Alternatively, he classified them into checks of misery (poverty, disease, hunger) and checks of vice. He also argued negatively that these checked population growth because population grew whenever they were removed.

Later editions of the *Essay* softened Malthus' system by adding to the checks of vice and misery a third check, that of moral restraint: sexual abstinence outside marriage and postponed marriage. This would enable societies to keep population under control without relying on vice and misery.

Malthus Has Been Misinterpreted

The "popular" version of Malthus' population theory quite obviously bears virtually no resemblance to the reality. Malthus did not say that population actually grows geometrically—only that it could, if unconstrained. He did not say that there will eventually be a disastrous famine to reduce excess population to what the food supply can support. Rather, checks on population growth always operate to keep population growth at a supportable pace. In Malthus' own writing, there is no "Malthusian trap" of population outrunning food supply and triggering a famine. Those who argue that he said these things have simply got him wrong.

It is a commonplace that Malthus has been refuted because he failed to anticipate the "green revolution" of high-yield strains of hybrid grains and other agricultural improvements. Stephen Moore [a senior follow at the libertarian Cato Institute] and [economist] Julian Simon, for instance, had it that

Malthus made a "dreary and world famous prediction that food supplies would run out" but never envisioned the green revolution, which "proves Malthus wrong." No, it doesn't. Europe's population had grown enormously since Roman times, Malthus observed, because "the industry of the inhabitants has made these countries produce a greater quantity of human subsistence." He deemed it undeniable that "population constantly bears a regular proportion to the food that the earth is made to produce." Later, Malthus reiterated that while means of subsistence limit population growth, "population does invariably increase when the means of subsistence increase." Far from refuting him, our ability to feed more people thanks to the green revolution readily squares with what he actually said.

The mainstream version of Malthus, then, is an ill-informed caricature and is disturbingly revealing about the standards of scholarship and research now prevailing. The writers on both sides who concocted this "Malthus" either never read the *Essay* themselves, relying instead on inaccurate secondary sources, or did read it but misunderstood or falsified what they read. However it happened, these treatments are untrustworthy. . . .

Malthus Remains Important

So Malthus is widely misrepresented; but is he still relevant? Yes, it turns out, he is.

Population studies writer Jack Parsons points out that much empirical evidence supports Malthus' claim that unchecked population growth has a doubling time of twenty-five years. Had population grown freely since Malthus' time, with eight doublings in two centuries, it would be three hundred billion now. "The fact that we have 'only' six billions, one-fiftieth (2 percent) of the theoretical figure, shows that some extremely powerful checks must have been operating," Parsons observes shrewdly.

Some, of course, are checks Malthus posited: war, pestilence, famine. But a revolution in beliefs and priorities in the advanced industrialized nations has generated additional, unanticipated checks. Affluence has retarded, rather than increased, fertility, as many parents have made a trade-off between having more children and giving their families a higher standard of living. Also, although the passion between the sexes remains strong, widespread valuation of leisure and self-actualization over duties such as parenthood, the sexual revolution, and the resultant popularization of contraception and abortion mean that it far less frequently yields children. Financial pressure and feminist encouragement of careers for women have led many women into the labor force. All these have combined to depress birthrates in all developed countries below the replacement level of 2.1 births per woman.

Population and the Land

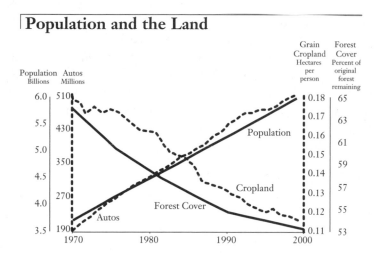

World Watch, March/April 2000.

So the core of Malthus' theory as Malthus himself stated it holds up: checks constantly operate to keep population growth supportable. Though the check of misery has weakened in industrialized countries, powerful new checks have replaced it: affluence, the sexual revolution, women's liberation, and so on. And, tragically, the checks of misery still operate in the LDCs.

Moreover, Malthus remains right in a more fundamental sense. Recall that he meant his *Essay* to debunk utopians: the need for constantly operating checks on population makes a utopian society impossible. Indeed, he devoted several of his later chapters specifically to debunking the notions of limitless improvement and attainment of an ideal society.

For example, Malthus observed that Condorcet had inferred from improvements in medicine, diet, and such that man was organically perfectible and that longevity would so increase as to become "indefinite," meaning either increasing without limit or increasing beyond any assignable lifespan. While "observable effects" of such improvements give grounds for this belief, Malthus retorted, the fact that one cannot assign a fixed limit to human longevity does not mean that it can increase indefinitely. He argued by analogy to breeding sheep for small heads and legs, which obviously could not be reduced without limit: "Though I may not be able . . . to mark the limit at which further improvement will stop, I can very easily mention a point at which it will not arrive." Even if such breeding continued forever, a sheep's head and legs could never be made as small as a rat's. The error, he concluded, was in "not discriminating between a small improvement, the limit of which is undefined, and an improvement really unlimited."

Limits to Improvement

Malthus' essential point, then, is that the world is limited and limits human possibilities; therefore, unlimited improvement and a perfect society are unattainable. This is as true now as it was in his day.

Modern, fossil fuel–based agriculture has greatly increased agricultural yields through machinery, nitrogen fertilizers (derived from natural gas), pesticides, monocultural-crop planting, and massive irrigation and groundwater pumping. But this came at the price of dependence upon a continued supply of cheap, abundant oil and natural gas. A consensus is emerging among petroleum geologists that the world's oil output will peak in this decade, then irreversibly decline, with natural gas output projected to peak around 2020. Other hydrocarbons such as heavy oil might make up the deficiency, but output so far is small. Smaller supplies of costlier petroleum will hamper our ability to feed growing populations. North Korea's recent famine is an awful warning of modern agriculture's vulnerability to breakdown;

when fuel and fertilizer supplies collapsed, three million North Koreans starved to death.

Another compelling limit is being approached: water supplies. No substitute for water exists, and three major food-growing areas—America's southern Great Plains (which help make America the world's largest wheat exporter), the Punjab in India, and the North China Plain (source of a third of China's grain harvest)—are rapidly depleting the groundwater on which they depend. North Africa and the Middle East are experiencing both rapid population growth and water shortages, forcing them to import grain. Iran and Egypt now import over 40 percent of their grain consumption. Water shortages are resulting in worldwide grain consumption outrunning output.

China's government has repeatedly cited water as the biggest constraint on China's economic growth and development. Overpumping has substantially drained the North China Plain's shallow aquifer, forcing the Chinese to tap the deep aquifer, which contains prehistoric water that cannot be replaced. Clearly, this is unsustainable; equally clearly, China will soon be forced to make massive grain imports.

Roughly half of U.S. agricultural output is currently exported, but the United States will soon hit a ceiling on its ability to feed a rising and more affluent world population. As agricultural historian John Opie observes, the old Dust Bowl area of Nebraska, Kansas, Oklahoma, and Texas has been turned into a global breadbasket by pumping groundwater from the underlying Ogallala aquifer to irrigate the fields. Unfortunately, this water, like that of the deep aquifer under the North China Plain, is largely unrenewable "fossil water," isolated from its sources thousands of years ago. One-third of the Ogallala's water is already gone, and it is currently being drained ten or more times faster than it is being replenished. According to the Texas Water Development Board, in 1997, for example, 6,231,000 acre-feet of water was removed from the Ogallala, while it was recharged with only 438,910 acre-feet. "Pumping the Ogallala remains an unrepeatable and irreversible experiment in continuous depletion," Opie warns, pointing out that at current rates of consumption the Ogallala will not last another fifty years; it can at most supply one more prosperous generation. What then?

Some writers—eerily reminiscent of the utopians whom Malthus refuted—have argued that with globalization and computer technology, we are on the verge of unprecedented affluence. But our way of life depends on cheap fossil fuels and water, and the disappearance of both will increasingly constrain our prospects. This is not to say that disaster is inevitable, merely that these euphoric predictions are as unlikely as Godwin's and Condorcet's.

Like Malthus, we cannot say what the limit on further improvement will be, but we can describe "a point at which it will not arrive": a world of simultaneous rising population and universal prosperity and affluence at levels undreamed of now, in which things like oil, natural gas, and groundwater will no longer matter. On the deepest level, then, Malthus will be vindicated after all.

| *"The greatest threat to the planet is not too
| many people, but too much statism."*

Population Growth Does Not Cause Environmental Problems

Stephen Moore

In 1789 English economist Thomas Malthus predicted that the world's food supply would not increase at a rate adequate to meet the needs of an ever-growing population. Stephen Moore contends in the following viewpoint that Malthus was mistaken and that an increasing population does not pose a threat to the environment. According to Moore, adherents of the population-control movement are wrong to believe that the world would be better served if families were limited to two children. He maintains that the world has more than enough food and land for 12 billion or more people. Moore is a senior fellow at the Cato Institute, a libertarian public policy research foundation, and a contributing editor to *National Review*.

As you read, consider the following questions:
1. What percentage of the children in Chinese orphanages is female, according to Moore?
2. In the author's opinion, when did the modern population-control movement begin?
3. Why are government-funded population programs counterproductive, in Moore's view?

At a Washington reception, the conversation turned to the merits of small families. One woman volunteered that she had just read Bill McKibben's environmental tome, *Maybe One*, on the benefits of single-child families. She claimed to have found it "ethically compelling." I chimed in: "Even one child may put too much stress on our fragile ecosystem. McKibben says 'maybe one.' I say, why not none?" The response was solemn nods of agreement, and even some guilt-ridden whispers between husbands and wives.

McKibben's acclaimed book is a tribute to the theories of British economist Thomas Malthus. [In 1799] Malthus—the original dismal scientist—wrote that "the power of population is . . . greater than the power in the earth to produce subsistence for man." McKibben's application of this idea was to rush out and have a vasectomy. He urges his fellow greens to do the same—to make single-child families the "cultural norm" in America.

Now, with the United Nations proclaiming that [in October 1999] we will surpass the demographic milestone of 6 billion people, the environmental movement and the media can be expected to ask: Do we really need so many people? [An] AP headline lamented: "Century's growth leaves Earth crowded—and noisy." Seemingly, Malthus has never had so many apostles.

The Rise of Population Control

In a rational world, Malthusianism would not be in a state of intellectual revival, but thorough disrepute. After all, virtually every objective trend is running in precisely the opposite direction of what the widely acclaimed Malthusians of the 1960s—from Lester Brown to Paul Ehrlich to the Club of Rome[1]—predicted. Birth rates around the world are lower today than at any time in recorded history. Global per capita food production is much higher than ever before. The "energy crisis" is now such a distant memory that oil is virtually the cheapest liquid on earth. These facts, collectively, have wrecked the credibility of the population-bomb propagandists.

Yet the population-control movement is gaining steam. It

1. an organization that studies the environment, economics, and other global issues

has won the hearts and wallets of some of the most influential leaders inside and outside government today. Malthusianism has evolved into a multi-billion-dollar industry and a political juggernaut.

Today, through the U.S. Agency for International Development (AID), the State Department, and the World Bank, the federal government pumps some 350 million tax dollars a year into population-containment activities. The Clinton administration would be spending at least twice that amount if not for the efforts of two Republican congressmen, Chris Smith of New Jersey and Todd Tiahrt of Kansas, who have managed to cut off funding for the most coercive birth-reduction initiatives.

Defenders of the U.N. Population Fund (UNFPA) and other such agencies insist that these programs "protect women's reproductive freedom," "promote the health of mothers," and "reduce infant mortality." Opponents of international "family planning," particularly Catholic organizations, are tarred as anti-abortion fanatics who want to deprive poor women of safe and cheap contraception. A 1998 newspaper ad by Planned Parenthood, entitled "The Right Wing Coup in Family Planning," urged continued USAID funding by proclaiming: "The very survival of women and children is at stake in this battle." Such rhetoric is truly Orwellian, given that the entire objective of government-sponsored birth-control programs has been to invade couples' "reproductive rights" in order to limit family size. The crusaders have believed, from the very outset, that coercion is necessary in order to restrain fertility and avert global eco-collapse.

The consequences of this crusade are morally atrocious. Consider the one-child policy in China. Some 10 million to 20 million Chinese girls are demographically "missing" today because of "sex-selective abortion of female fetuses, female infant mortality (through infanticide or abandonment), and selective neglect of girls ages 1 to 4," according to a 1996 U.S. Census Bureau report. Girls account for over 90 percent of the inmates of Chinese orphanages—where children are left to die from neglect. . . .

Coercive practices are spreading to other countries. [Pro-life activist] Brian Clowes writes in the *Yale Journal of Ethics* that coercion has been used to promote family planning in at least 35 developing countries. Peru has started to use sterilization as a means of family planning, and doctors have to meet sterilization quotas or risk losing their jobs. The same is true in Mexico. In disease-ridden African countries such as Nigeria and Kenya, hospitals often lack even the most rudimentary medical care, but are stocked to the rafters with boxes of contraceptives stamped "UNFPA" and "USAID." UNFPA boasts that, thanks to its shipments, more than 80 percent of the women in Haiti have access to contraceptives; this is apparently a higher priority than providing access to clean water, which is still unavailable to more than half of the Haitian population.

Two Misconceptions

Population-control groups like Zero Population Growth and International Planned Parenthood have teamed up with pro-choice women in Congress—led by Carolyn Maloney of New York, Cynthia McKinney of Georgia, and Connie Morella of Maryland—to try to secure $60 million in U.S. funding for UNFPA [for 2000 and 2001]. Maloney pledges, "I'm going to do whatever it takes to restore funding for [UNFPA in 1999]."

Support for this initiative is based on two misconceptions. The first is the excessively optimistic view that (in the words of a *Chicago Tribune* report) "one child zealotry in China is fading." The Population Research Institute's Steve Mosher, an authority on Chinese population activities, retorts, "This fantasy that things are getting better in China has been the constant refrain of the one-child apologists for at least the past twenty years." In fact, after UNFPA announced in 1997 that it was going back into China, state councillor Peng Peiyun defiantly announced, "China will not slacken our family-planning policy in the next century."

The second myth is that UNFPA has always been part of the solution, and has tried to end China's one-child policy. We are told that it is pushing Beijing toward more "female friendly" family planning. This, too, is false. UNFPA has actually given an award to China for its effectiveness in population-control activities—activities far from female-friendly. Worse,

UNFPA's executive director, Nafis Sadik, is, like her predecessors, a longtime apologist for the China program and even denies that it is coercive. She is on record as saying—falsely—that "the implementation of the policy is purely voluntary. There is no such thing as a license to have a birth."

The Degradation Narrative

New Scientist: Where did the environment come into your thinking on population?

Betsy Hartmann: I got concerned that conflicts over resources such as forests and land were being framed so that population pressure was seen as the main culprit. A variety of groups, including foundations that fund population work, were linking population and environment issues directly to national security. This seemed like a dangerous mix, especially when it got tied up with the growing anti-immigrant movement in the US, and maybe now in Europe, too.

But isn't population pressure a real environmental issue?

It's more than an issue, it's an ideology. Ever since colonial times, Westerners have had what I call a degradation narrative. It says that poor peasants having too many children causes population pressures that degrade the environment and cause more poverty. It is the basic story that many Western environmentalists still tell. And it is now being extended to explain not just the loss of rainforests and species, but also migration and violent conflicts round the world.

Betsy Hartmann, *New Scientist*, February 22, 2003.

Despite UNFPA's track record, don't be surprised if Congress winds up re-funding it. The past 20 years may have demonstrated the intellectual bankruptcy of the population controllers, but their coffers have never been more flush. American billionaires, past and present, have devoted large parts of their fortunes to population control. The modern-day population-control movement dates to 1952, when John D. Rockefeller returned from a trip to Asia convinced that the teeming masses he saw there were the single greatest threat to the earth's survival. He proceeded to divert hundreds of millions of dollars from his foundation to the goal of population stabilization. He was followed by David Packard (co-founder of Hewlett-Packard), who created a $9 billion foundation whose top priority was reducing world population.

Today, these foundations are joined by organizations ranging from Zero Population Growth (ZPG) to Negative Population Growth (which advocates an optimal U.S. population size of 150 million—120 million fewer than now) to Planned Parenthood to the Sierra Club. The combined budget of these groups approaches $1 billion.

Extremist Views

These organizations tend to be extremist. Take ZPG. Its board of directors passed a resolution declaring that "parenthood is not an inherent right but a privilege" granted by the state, and that "every American family has a right to no more than two children."

"Population growth is analogous to a plague of locusts," says [media mogul] Ted Turner, a major source of population-movement funding. "What we have on this earth today is a plague of people. Nature did not intend for there to be as many people as there are." Turner has also penned "The Ted Commandments," which include "a promise to have no more than two children or no more than my nation suggests." He recently reconsidered his manifesto, and now believes that the voluntary limit should be even lower—just one child. In Turner's utopia, there are no brothers, sisters, aunts, or uncles.

Turner's $1 billion donation to the U.N. is a pittance compared with the fortunes that Warren Buffett (net worth $36 billion) and Bill Gates (net worth roughly $100 billion) may bestow on the cause of population control. Buffett has announced repeatedly that he views overpopulation as one of the greatest crises in the world today. Earlier [in 1999,] Gates and his wife contributed an estimated $7 billion to their foundation, of which the funding of population programs is one of five major initiatives.

This is a massive misallocation of funds, for the simple reason that the overpopulation crisis is a hoax. It is true that world population has tripled over the last century. But the explanation is both simple and benign: First, life expectancy—possibly the best overall numerical measure of human well-being—has almost doubled in the last 100 years, and the years we are tacking on to life are both more active and more productive. Second, people are wealthier—they can afford better health care, better diets, and a cleaner environment. As a result, infant-mortality rates have declined nearly tenfold in this century. As the late Julian Simon often explained, population growth is a sign of mankind's greatest triumph—our gains against death.

We are told that this good news is really bad news, because human numbers are soon going to bump up against the planet's "carrying capacity."

The World Has Abundant Resources

Pessimists worry that man is procreating as uncontrollably as [ecologist and researcher] John B. Calhoun's famous Norwegian rats, which multiply until they die off from lack of sustenance. Bill McKibben warns that "we are adding another New York City every month, a Mexico every year, and almost another India every decade."

But a closer look shows that these fears are unfounded. Fact: If every one of the 6 billion of us resided in Texas, there would be room enough for every family of four to have a house and one-eighth of an acre of land—the rest of the globe would be vacant. (True, if population growth continued, some of these people would eventually spill over into Oklahoma.) In short, the population bomb has been defused. The birth rate in developing countries has plummeted from just over 6 children per couple in 1950 to just over 3 today. The major explanation for smaller family sizes, even in China, has been economic growth. The Reaganites were right on the mark when, in 1984, they proclaimed this truth to a distraught U.N. delegation in Mexico City. (The policy they enunciated has been memorably expressed in the phrase "capitalism is by far the best contraceptive.") The fertility rate in the developed world has fallen from 3.3 per couple in 1950 to 1.6 today. These low fertility rates presage declining populations.

If, for example, Japan's birth rate is not raised at some point, in 500 years there will be only about 15 Japanese left on the planet.

Other Malthusian worries are similarly wrongheaded. Global food prices have fallen by half since 1950, even as world population has doubled. The dean of agricultural economists, D. Gale Johnson of the University of Chicago, has documented "a dramatic decline in famines" in the last 50 years. Fewer than half as many people die of famine each year now than did a century ago—despite a near-quadrupling of the population. Enough food is now grown in the world to provide every resident of the planet with almost four pounds of food a day. [In 1997, 1998, and 1999] global food production has reached new heights. Overeating is fast becoming the globe's primary dietary malady. "It's amazing to say, but our problem is becoming overnutrition," Ho Zhiqiuan, a Chinese nutrition expert, . . . told *National Geographic.* "Today in China obesity is becoming common."

Millions are still hungry, and famines continue to occur—but these are the result of government policies or political malice, not inadequate global food production. As the International Red Cross has reported, "the loss of access to food resources [during famines] is generally the result of intentional acts" by governments.

Even if the apocalyptic types are correct and population grows to 12 billion in the 21st century, so what? Assuming that human progress and scientific advancement continue as they have, and assuming that the global march toward capitalism is not reversed, those 12 billion people will undoubtedly be richer, healthier, and better fed than the 6 billion of us alive today. After all, we 6 billion are much richer, healthier, and better fed than the 1 billion who lived in 1800 or the 2 billion alive in 1920.

Governments Are a Greater Problem

The greatest threat to the planet is not too many people, but too much statism. The Communists, after all, were the greatest polluters in history.

Economist Mikhail Bernstam has discovered that market-based economies are about two to three times more energy-efficient than Communist, socialist, Maoist, or "Third Way" economies. Capitalist South Korea has three times the population density of socialist North Korea, but South Koreans are well fed while 250,000 North Koreans have starved to death in the [1990s].

Government-funded population programs are actually

counterproductive, because they legitimize command-and-control decision-making. As the great development economist Alan Rufus Waters puts it, "Foreign aid used for population activities gives enormous resources and control apparatus to the local administrative elite and thus sustains the authoritarian attitudes corrosive to the development process."

This approach usually ends up making poor people poorer, because it distracts developing nations from their most pressing task, which is market reform. When Mao's China[2] established central planning and communal ownership of agriculture, tens of millions of Chinese peasants starved to death. In 1980, after private ownership was established, China's agricultural output doubled in just ten years. If Chinese leaders over the past 30 years had concentrated on rapid privatization and market reform, it's quite possible that economic development would have decreased birth rates every bit as rapidly as the one-child policy.

An Assault on the Importance of Humans

The problem with trying to win this debate with logic and an arsenal of facts is that modern Malthusianism is not a scientific theory at all. It's a religion, in which the assertion that mankind is overbreeding is accepted as an article of faith. I . . . participated in a debate before an anti-population group called Carrying Capacity Network, at which one scholar informed me that man's presence on the earth is destructive because Homo sapiens is the only species without a natural predator. It's hard to argue with somebody who despairs because mankind is alone at the top of the food chain.

At its core, the population-control ethic is an assault on the principle that every human life has intrinsic value. Malthusian activists tend to view human beings neither as endowed with intrinsic value, nor even as resources, but primarily as consumers of resources.

2. Mao Zedong founded the People's Republic of China.

Periodical Bibliography

The following articles have been selected to supplement the diverse views presented in this chapter.

Ronald Bailey	"Earth Day, Then and Now," *Reason*, May 2000.
Congressional Digest	"Ocean Policy," September 2003.
Mary H. Cooper	"Threatened Fisheries," *CQ Researcher*, August 2, 2002.
Betsy Hartmann	"The Greening of Hate," *New Scientist*, February 22, 2003.
Steven Hayward	"America's Environmental Rebirth," *World & I*, March 2002.
David Hosansky	"Mass Extinction," *CQ Researcher*, September 15, 2000.
Issues and Controversies On File	"Global Warming Update," April 25, 2003.
Gordon Laird	"Losing the Cool," *Mother Jones*, March/April 2002.
Eugene Linden	"Condition Critical," *Time*, April/May 2000.
Jim Motavalli	"Balancing Act," *E: The Environmental Magazine*, November 2000.
Robert H. Nelson	"Suppose the Globe *Is* Warming," *Liberty*, February 2003.
Rachel Rivera and Nigel Holmes	"A Pocket Guide to the Environmental Millennium," *Amicus Journal*, Winter 2000.
Joel Schwartz	"Clearing the Air," *Regulation*, Summer 2003.
William K. Stevens	"Global Warming: The Contrarian View," *New York Times*, February 29, 2000.

CHAPTER 2

How Can Pollution Best Be Prevented?

Chapter Preface

Automobiles are to blame for much of America's pollution woes. According to scientists Michael Brower and Warren Leon, in their book *The Consumer's Guide to Effective Environmental Choices*, cars and light trucks create 45 percent of toxic air emissions, with "the average new car . . . responsible for about 2 metric tons of carbon emissions each year." Consequently one of the best ways to prevent air pollution might be by building automobiles that create fewer emissions. However, cars with all-electric engines have not turned out to be a panacea—General Motors pulled its EV1 automobile off the market in 2003, and Ford ceased researching electric vehicles a year earlier. On the other hand, hybrid automobiles, which run on a combination of gasoline and electricity, may turn out to be an important advance in the fight against pollution.

Hybrid vehicles primarily run on electric batteries, with the car receiving extra power from the internal combustion engine (ICE) as needed, such as when it needs to accelerate on a freeway. The cars recharge their batteries during braking, making these vehicles more convenient than the EV1 and other all-electric automobiles, which have batteries that require recharging every fifty to seventy miles. Moreover, their fuel efficiency is superior to most ICE vehicles; makers of hybrid cars claim that their vehicles can get as much as sixty-eight miles per gallon, although studies by consumer and automobile magazines have found that the mpg is a lower, but still respectable, forty to forty-eight. Because hybrid vehicles use less gasoline than traditional cars, they release fewer pollutants into the air.

Despite these advantages, hybrid vehicles have yet to make significant inroads into the American market. As of early 2004, only three models were available for purchase in the United States: the Toyota Prius, and the Honda Civic and Insight. However, Ford, Daimler Chrysler, and Chevrolet have announced plans to release hybrid vehicles in the coming years. Sales are still small—only thirty-six thousand of these vehicles were sold in the United States in 2002. Sales may rise as competition brings down prices and hybrid versions of SUVs, trucks, and other popular types of automobiles are manufactured.

As long as automobiles remain the primary source of transportation for Americans, car companies will need to develop vehicles that are less environmentally destructive. Hybrid vehicles may help prevent pollution and create a healthier environment. In the following chapter the authors consider several other ways to prevent pollution. Ensuring that Americans can enjoy clean air and water is an important goal for the twenty-first century.

"Thanks largely to the [Clean Water] Act, we have made considerable progress in cleaning up our nation's waterways."

Government Regulations Help Prevent Water Pollution

Sierra Club

In the following viewpoint the Sierra Club, one of the oldest and most influential environmental organizations in the United States, argues that government regulations such as the Clean Water Act of 1972 have helped improve the quality of water in America. The organization cites the decrease in toxic discharges and sewage entering bays, rivers, and lakes in New England and the Midwest as proof that the Clean Water Act has made these and other areas safe for tourists and fishermen.

As you read, consider the following questions:

1. By what percentage has sewage in the Narragansett Bay been reduced since 1972, according to the Sierra Club?
2. According to the organization, how much money is generated each year by Lake Erie's sport fishing industry?
3. How many gallons of wastewater are treated daily, as stated by the Sierra Club?

Thirty years ago, our nation's leaders set a reasonable goal: Make all waters of the United States safe for swimming and fishing. . . . Today about 60% of our rivers and 55% of our lakes are safe for swimming and fishing compared to just 36% in 1970.

The Clean Water Act: The Key to Cleaner Lakes, Rivers and Coastal Waters

In 1969, a rail car passing over the Cuyahoga River set fire to a huge oil slick floating downstream. The flaming river became a powerful symbol for the abysmal conditions of our nation's lakes and rivers. Boston Harbor was little more than a cesspool; Lake Erie was declared biologically dead; and cities that lined the Potomac, Hudson, Delaware and other major rivers simply dumped their raw sewage directly into the water. Growing public concern that uncontrolled pollution was making our waters unsafe led to the passage of the Clean Water Act in 1972.

Thanks largely to the Act, we have made considerable progress in cleaning up our nation's waterways over the past three decades. Today, seals and porpoises swim off South Boston's Castle Island, fishermen routinely catch lobsters, and tourists enjoy pleasure cruises through the harbor. Many of America's urban waterfronts, including Cleveland's once-notorious "Flats," are experiencing a revival, and many once sewage-filled rivers are now safe for fishing, swimming and boating.

So why is the Bush administration asking us to settle for polluted waters? We can make all of our lakes, rivers, streams and wetlands healthy and safe.

In January, 2003, the Bush administration issued an immediate policy guidance that would remove protections from many of our small streams, ponds and wetlands that appear to be disconnected from major rivers and lakes. The administration also solicited public comment on a preliminary proposal to weaken Clean Water Act rules. According to the Environmental Protection Agency [EPA], the guidance alone places at risk 20% of the United States' remaining wetlands, some 20 million acres. Ultimately, a majority of the nation's stream-miles could lose Clean Water Act protections.

Protecting Their Treasure: Narragansett Bay, Rhode Island and Massachusetts

The Past

For hundreds of years, communities dumped raw sewage into the [Narragansett] Bay, triggering cholera and typhoid epidemics in the 1800's. Despite improvements in the 1950's and 60's, sewer systems were over-flowing and dumping 2.2 billion gallons of untreated sewage into Narragansett Bay and its tributaries each year. Frequently, the water was so dirty it was unsafe to swim at local beaches. By the 1970's, centuries of industrial activity, the construction of upstream dams, development and pollution had crippled Narragansett Bay.

Around 40% of the Narragansett Bay's wetlands have been filled, allowing more pollutants to flow into the Bay and resulting in an increased flood risk. Fishing was frequently restricted due to pollution. In 1946, for example, the entire Bay was closed to shellfishing due to waste contamination.

The Present

Thanks to limits on industrial pollution put in place by the Clean Water Act, the level of toxic discharges into the Bay has dropped by 90% over the last 30 years. To comply with the Clean Water Act, cities used federal funding to improve their sewage treatment facilities along Narragansett Bay. Conservative estimates indicate that the amount of sewage entering the Bay has been reduced by 60% since the Clean Water Act was enacted.

John Torgan, the baykeeper from Save the Bay, a local non-profit organization working to protect and restore Narragansett Bay, explains that Rhode Islanders "don't have gold, don't have diamonds; we have the Bay." Residents recognize the Bay as a crucial natural resource, essential for the local economy and necessary for many plants and animals.

The Clean Water Act has been a key tool in protecting the Bay and it has empowered local citizens to defend their right to clean water. Save the Bay and other citizen groups have frequently used powers given them under the Clean Water Act to ensure that the government fulfills its responsibilities in water protection, including limiting pollution from industry.

Despite progress in Narragansett Bay, the cleanup job is

Three Leading Sources of Water Pollution

Rank	Rivers	Lakes	Estuaries
1	Agricultural runoff	Agricultural runoff	Agricultural runoff
2	Municipal point sources	Municipal point sources	Municipal point sources
3	Stream/ habitat changes	Urban runoff	Agricultural runoff

Environmental Protection Agency.

far from over. Excessive nitrogen contained in wastewater and runoff, as well as combined sewer overflows in the upper areas of the Bay, continue to threaten its health.

Cleaning Up Ohio's Licking River

The Past

By the 1980's, high levels of health-threatening bacteria in the Licking River made it unsafe for boating, much less swimming. From 1979 until 1983, the local sewage treatment plant repeatedly violated its legal limits established under the Clean Water Act. The plant was in violation for almost the entire year in 1983, in large part due to discharges of toxic chemicals by a local industry, Owens-Corning Fiberglass. These chemicals upset the normal cleanup process at the sewage treatment plant, allowing untreated sewage to run into the river. One of these spills alone killed 80,000 fish, turned the water black and made the river stink of raw sewage.

The Present

Clean water rules should have prevented any discharges of toxic chemicals from ruining the operation of the sewage treatment plant, but the State of Ohio was failing to enforce the law.

A local resident, Ernie Grimm, went to court to force the Ohio EPA to enforce the law—and he won.

The Ohio EPA found both the municipal treatment plant and Owens-Corning in violation and ordered a $26 million renovation of the city's sewage-treatment plant, mostly funded through a Clean Water Act grant, and a $1 million toxic chemical treatment system at Owens-Corning.

Thanks to these improvements, Owens-Corning is now complying with clean water safeguards, and water in the river is clear. Great progress has been made; most of the river is now clean. People can now safely swim, fish and boat on the Licking River.

Breathing Life Back into the Great Lakes

The Past

The Great Lakes contain 95% of all surface fresh water in the United States. More than 35 million people living in the region depend upon the Great Lakes for clean water. But decades of urban and industrial pollution threatened this critical resource. Lake Erie was declared biologically dead in the 1960's; by the early 1970's, the public realized the threat to all the lakes.

The Present

Thanks to the Clean Water Act and cooperative efforts between the United States and Canada, the Great Lakes are much improved. The amount of toxic substances entering the lakes has been greatly reduced. The cleanup of sewage treatment plants has dramatically reduced the amount of raw sewage spilling into the lakes, sewage which once caused massive algae blooms and fish kills. Today, Lake Erie is home to a thriving sports fishing industry that generates $11 billion annually.

Still, there is a long way to go before the Great Lakes can be considered truly clean. Warnings against eating fish remain in place on all of the lakes. Along the Great Lakes, the United States and Canada still must clean up 42 toxic sites.

The Clean Water Act: One of Our Most Successful Environmental Laws

Cleaner water has increased the size and variety of fish populations in our waters—helping angling grow into a sport enjoyed by 35 million Americans and creating an industry that generates $38 billion annually.

Striped bass stocks in every coastal state from Maine to North Carolina have been declared fully recovered.

In 1972, the country lost an estimated 450,000 acres of wetlands each year. Today, losses are estimated at about one-fourth that rate.

More than 1 billion pounds of toxic chemicals are removed from wastewater each year.

32 trillion gallons of wastewater are treated each day.

More than 16 billion pounds of oxygen-depleting pollution are removed from wastewater each year.

Thousands of cities have received federal funds to construct and expand wastewater treatment facilities that prevent or reduce the discharge of pollutants into the nation's waters.

The number of Americans served by sewage treatment facilities has more than doubled in the last 30 years.

Protect Your Local Stream, Pond or Wetland

Send a letter to the editor of your local newspaper about this issue. For a sample letter, visit the Sierra Club Clean Water website at http://www.sierraclub.org/cleanwater/get_involved. asp.

Contact your Senators and member of Congress. Urge them to protect the waters in your region by opposing the Bush administration's efforts to weaken Clean Water Act rules. To contact them via email, visit http://whistler.sierraclub.org/action/actionindex.jsp.

Stay informed about the Bush administration's threat to clean water. Visit the Sierra Club's website at http://www.sierraclub.org/cleanwater. Join the Sierra Club's clean water email list by sending an email to clean.water@sierraclub.org.

Help protect a stream or wetland: Join a local water-monitoring group to help protect a stream or wetland in your community. To find a group near you, check this website: http://www.epa.gov/owow/monitoring/vol.html.

For more information: Contact Ed Hopkins at ed.hopkins @sierraclub.org or 202-675-7908 or Robin Mann at robin. mann@sierraclub.org.

| "Federal bungling on local sewage control
| goes back to the enshrined Clean Water
| Act of 1972."

Government Regulations Do Not Prevent Water Pollution

Steve Seachman

Government regulations, such as the Clean Water Act, have failed to make America's oceans and lakes cleaner, Steve Seachman contends in the following viewpoint. He asserts that beaches are frequently closed because of unsanitary conditions and that millions of Americans have become sick from sanitary-sewage overflows. According to Seachman, the federal government, in particular the Environmental Protection Agency, is to blame for the poor quality of America's water because it has not targeted the urban sewage treatment facilities that are the sources of the unclean water. He concludes that cities should consider privatizing their wastewater systems if they want to have clean water. Seachman is an environmental engineer and freelance writer.

As you read, consider the following questions:

1. According to a survey cited by Seachman, the United States had what number of combined days of beach closings and advisories against swimming in 2000?
2. In Seachman's opinion, why is there no independent watchdog that tracks beach closures?
3. What problems arise with sewage treatment systems that have separate storm and sanitary lines, according to the author?

C hances are, at this very moment, a family is arriving at some U.S. shoreline ready to spend a week relaxing at the beach. But before mom, dad and the kids can get their feet warm in the sand, a sign confronts them: "Beach closed. No swimming allowed." As the children slouch back to the car, a parent tries to console them. "At least the hotel has a swimming pool, and there's always next year." And so it goes.

Similar routines are played out for real thousands of times each year in this country. And the culprits—those who dump veritable rivers of untreated toilet water and city-street runoff into the nearest ditch or bay—aren't some gang of industrial ogres. They happen to be your local government sewer-system operators.

This is not supposed to be happening. Not in America, at least. Not after Congress passed the expansive Clean Water Act that predicted water pollution would be entirely "eliminated by 1985." Yet it does happen, and quite often. And federal officials don't just know about it; they are actively rewarding the worst offenders with more tax dollars.

Apparently, official Washington doesn't even think that citizens need to be informed about this matter. Congress and the Environmental Protection Agency (EPA) currently shield these government polluters from the popular "Right to Know" program of annual emission reporting to which industry is subject.

Beach Closings

According to the Natural Resources Defense Council (NRDC), which reviewed surveys from 2,251 ocean and lake beaches, the nation had at least 11,270 combined days of beach closings and advisories against swimming during 2000. The group's annual *Testing the Waters* report notes there were an additional 98 extended closings and advisories that persisted for at least six weeks.

This problem has lurked beneath the surface for years. Since 1989 (when less data were available) there have been at least 1,000 days reported annually in which swimming was restricted. From 1997 to 1999 there were more than 17,500 such days. And public officials usually don't close popular bathing areas unless waters are pretty disgusting—where one exposure to the bacteria- and virus-laden swill could give you nausea, skin rash, diarrhea or worse.

The June 12, 2000, issue of *U.S. News & World Report* mentioned a preliminary study done for the EPA that estimated more than 1 million Americans get sick each year from sanitary-sewage overflows. . . . In a previous brief disclosure, the EPA pitched similar figures—strictly as an opportunity, though, not a problem. Buried in a 1999 report to Congress, the EPA claimed that "up to 500,000 cases of illness will be avoided annually" just by "reducing" storm-water pollution with its programs.

After years of public authorities keeping this issue mostly to themselves, NRDC's *Testing the Waters* series finally prompted federal regulators into action. In 1998, seven years after NRDC issued its premier edition, the EPA produced its first volume on the subject. But the federal beach reports couldn't be more bland. For example, the EPA's finding that 24 percent of reporting beaches in 1999 "were affected by an advisory or closure" is about as hyper as the normally ferocious agency ever gets. The EPA provides no comment to its assessment that "34 percent of beaches were monitored less than once per week." So, if the beach you're swimming in was just flooded with raw sewage yesterday, look out!

Since the EPA and the states don't track beach closures in any remotely consistent manner, it is hard to determine any trend. But it's clear that a significant problem has existed for some time. And it remains a nuisance today. But lacking a predictable corporate scapegoat, this widespread situation has received little attention.

Raw Sewage Discharge

The leading cause of U.S. beach closings, according to NRDC and the EPA, is mismanagement of sewage-handling systems and urban storm-water runoff. Both utilities almost always are run by local governments, with partial funding and sporadic oversight typically kicked in from the state and federal levels. State and local agencies also manage beach functions in most cases. So in the end, there is no one left to be an independent watchdog.

Based on the limited data available on the topic, St. Louis

appears to be at rock bottom, spilling an average of 26 billion gallons of untreated sewage and storm water during 106 "overflow" events each year. Portland, Ore., is a close second with 100 discharges but only 3.4 billion gallons of annual pollution. Chicago, Pittsburgh, Boston, Indianapolis and Cleveland typically experience from 10 to 70 untreated bypasses, according to an April 2000 study by the Milwaukee Metropolitan Sewage District. (All of these cities have some sort of abatement plan in the works and claim that dumping will diminish—in 10 or 20 years.) But as of today, citizens from San Diego to Buffalo to Miami and many other communities face thousands of smaller but still putrid events each year. And these polluters rarely even get a slap on the wrist.

A Fraudulent Act

The Clean Water Act (CWA) of 1972—acclaimed as "the American environmental movement's single most important achievement"—isn't up to the job. In fact, to put it *very* bluntly, the CWA is something of a fraud. More accurately known as the Federal Water Pollution Control Act, this law set in place a regulatory system that does not and cannot promise verifiable environmental benefits. Instead of pinpointing problems and dealing with them directly and efficiently, it has been striking out blindly for almost thirty years, attacking with equal force both imagined and real waterquality problems, sometimes hitting, sometimes missing, but always gobbling up billions of dollars at a gulp.

Richard A. Halpern, *American Outlook*, November/December 2000.

Public officials in Washington admit to discharging raw sewage 60 to 70 times a year into the Potomac River and its tributaries. Although city leaders have had decades to fix the problems, the EPA offers nothing but praise. An EPA senior official, Lee Murphy, told a civil-engineering trade magazine in July 2001 that "D.C. is moving aggressively to address the issue." The *Engineering News-Record* reported that city managers could begin construction on a remedy as early as 2005.

In Iowa, an April 18 [2002] editorial in the *Des Moines Register* encouraged citizens to "use your own judgement," then dive head first into beaches soaked with human waste and farm leachate. It's a "reasonable risk," the paper adds. Under the state's new plan, if the waters are shown to have high bacteria counts for five samples in a 30-day period, warning signs of "Swimming Not Recommended" now will be posted in lieu of an all-out prohibition. Bathers at Iowa's 35 state beaches will be told to shower after swimming. And the state will avoid [2001's] embarrassment of frequent beach closures.

While similar affronts go on across the nation—right now, with direct adverse effects on the public—the environmental establishment is virtually silent. Green-lobby powerhouses such as the Sierra Club, Greenpeace and the rest are preoccupied with futuristic doomsday theories on global warming or fighting against vague dangers of free-trade "globalization." The antisewage folks at the NRDC spend most of their time with these anti-industry efforts, as well.

Why Sewage Is Still a Problem

Federal bungling on local sewage control goes back to the enshrined Clean Water Act of 1972, which laid a rather warped foundation. Prior to the early 1970s, it was common for cities and towns simply to dump raw sewage into the nearest waterway. Instead of simply establishing safe discharge limits for the EPA to enforce, the act's chief method of curbing this filthy habit was to shower local officials with free cash to upgrade their treatment systems or build new facilities altogether. The ongoing pork feast is up to $73 billion (not adjusted for inflation) to help reckless municipalities clean up their own messes. In return, federal officials get abundant opportunities for campaign kickbacks and patronage appointments.

Back when the grant program was created, at least the stated intentions were believed to be pointed in the right direction. In 1972, local governments discharged sewage that was completely untreated or had received only primary treatment (such as settling tanks) from 34 million residents. As of 1992, that figure had decreased to slightly more than 1 million.

That sounds great until you step back and consider how the sewage gets to a treatment facility in the first place: the sewer lines themselves. Many of these are rotting, if not ill-conceived from their beginning. About 880 communities serving more than 40 million people continue to rely on the pre–Civil War design of combining storm water and sanitary effluents in a single pipe. Whenever it rains a great deal, the double-duty conduits unload their mixed brew of waste via spill ports—called "combined sewer overflows"—into the closest body of water. The EPA figures that combined sewers discharge 1.2 trillion gallons of untreated sewage and storm water each year—equivalent to 18 days of flow from Niagara Falls.

Systems with separate storm and sanitary lines aren't necessarily much better. Urban storm water is loaded with bacteria, metals, gasoline and other chemicals. Vast amounts of tainted runoff are dumped into U.S. waters each year with absolutely no treatment.

Because of poor construction methods, many of the nation's sanitary sewer lines, perhaps all of them, leak badly. After a downpour, the crumbling pipes swell with infiltration and deluge the receiving treatment plant. The EPA quietly estimates that sanitary sewers overflow at least 40,000 times a year.

Washington Is Not the Answer

While any private company likely would face a multimillion-dollar penalty and its officials possible jail time for even one similar stunt, public-sector pigs slop it up with full immunity. The worst punishment the EPA ever dishes out to government violators is to fine the innocent taxpayers and give the sewage dumpers a hefty raise. As for municipal sewer rot, the EPA and some politicians are pushing for anywhere from $57 billion to $130 billion in new federal spending allegedly to fix the problem this time. In modern eco-speak, this is called paying polluters to pollute, which in any other case the EPA rightly would condemn.

To escape this pattern of failure, the first task should be immediately to add sewage plants to EPA's "Right to Know" program of annual emission reporting. Thanks to the pressures of public disclosure, industrial releases fell by nearly 50 percent in the first 10 years of reporting, which began in 1987. Similar results likely could be achieved for government polluters—if they are ever led out of the closet.

Bold communities that prefer clean water and lower taxes

should consider privatizing their wastewater systems. This means replacing municipal patronage dynasties with people accountable both to periodic competitive bidding and to oversight by independent regulators. Cities such as Milwaukee and Indianapolis have done it to various degrees, with much success.

Most importantly, towns and villages should stop looking to Washington for a handout. Polluting communities will have to decide for themselves if they would rather swim in their own sewage or do what it takes to fix their own problem.

"It would be . . . better to turn to sources of energy that do not emit greenhouse gases."

Renewable Energy Can Prevent Pollution

John R.E. Bliese

The greenhouse gases created by the burning of coal and oil pollute the air and may severely affect the global climate. In the following viewpoint John R.E. Bliese maintains that greenhouse gas emissions could be eliminated if people turned to renewable sources of energy. Bliese details several sources of this energy, including sun, wind, biomass (plant material and ethanol), and fuel cells. According to Bliese, renewable energy has gained in popularity throughout Europe and has great potential in the United States, particularly as the costs of these sources become comparable to that of fossil fuels. Bliese is an associate professor of communication studies at Texas Tech University.

As you read, consider the following questions:
1. Why does Bliese believe that no more nuclear power plants should be built?
2. According to the author, what percentage of Sweden's energy comes from biomass?
3. In Bliese's opinion why have fossil fuels remained inexpensive?

[O ne] way to reduce greenhouse gases is to reduce or, better, eliminate carbon in generating heat and electricity and powering our vehicles. There are many things that could be done. One is to switch from high-carbon to lower-carbon fuels in our power plants. Of the main fossil fuels now used, coal has the highest carbon content, oil has less, and natural gas has the least. Retiring older coal-burning plants and replacing them with natural gas power generation significantly lowers the amount of CO_2 released in producing a given amount of electricity or heat. A study of thirty-one states in the East concludes that if utilities switched from fuel oil to natural gas, their CO_2 emissions would be reduced by over 46 million tons per year at an average cost of $4.48 per ton reduced.

Where coal is used, the efficiency of power plants can be improved. Older coal-fired power plants now convert only 32 percent of the energy stored in their fuel into electricity. Newer technologies can increase that to 42 percent or so. This reduces the amount of CO_2 released from the production of any given amount of electricity. But coal is still a high-carbon fuel and as demand for power increases so will greenhouse gas emissions. (Natural gas wins out here too. The efficiency of a modern gas plant is 60 percent.)

Another way to increase efficiency is to locate electricity generating plants in places where their otherwise wasted heat can be used to make steam for heating, a process known as cogeneration, or combined heat and power (CHP). Industrial plants can also do their own cogeneration. Both the electricity and the otherwise lost heat can then be used productively. This is already done in many places in Europe. The efficiency of using the energy potential in the fuel goes way up—total system efficiencies of some cogeneration plants are well above 80 percent. But greenhouse gases are still emitted.

Sources of Cleaner Energy

It would be much better to turn to sources of energy that do not emit greenhouse gases at all or do not add to their concentrations in the atmosphere. Advocates from the nuclear power industry point out that fission reactions release no greenhouse gases, so building more reactors could replace a lot of fossil fuel. But of course nuclear power plants produce dangerous wastes of their own. We clearly should not build any more nuclear power plants until we have found a definitive solution to storing the industry's highly radioactive waste, which is extremely dangerous for thousands of years. Besides, because of the high investment costs and huge subsidies involved, expanding nuclear power production would be a most inefficient use of our money. As Amory Lovins [the cofounder of the resource policy center Rocky Mountain Institute] often reminds us, nuclear power in America "ate $1 trillion, yet delivers less energy than wood." Several other technologies, however, could be used.

More Affordable than Natural Gas

Claim: New natural gas power plants will provide cheaper energy than wind plants.

Responses:

• This is not likely at today's gas prices, and these prices are rising with time. At $3/MBTU, [millions of British Thermal Units] the fuel cost alone is 2.5 to 3¢/kWh [kilowatt-hour], and capital and O&M [operation and maintenance] costs add a comparable amount. And gas prices have spiked to over $10/MBTU in the past three years. Betting on low gas prices over the foreseeable future is highly risky, while energy costs from wind plants will be relatively stable over time.

• Gas price volatility is not going away. Planned power plant construction countrywide is nearly 100% gas fired and the success of these plans is heavily dependent on natural gas production meeting growing demand. The economics of these plants are based on low gas prices into the future. Witness the California power crisis and the impact of price volatility on the general health of our economy.

Ed DeMeo and Brian Parsons, "Some Common Misconceptions About Wind Power," Oregon Department of Energy, May 22, 2003. www.energy.state.or.us.

Solar power has enormous potential. Passive solar systems can heat buildings while producing no greenhouse gases at all. Space heat demand could be reduced by 90 percent or more in residential and commercial buildings by using passive solar designs and good insulation. The Rocky Mountain Institute building in Snowmass, Colorado, needs no furnace at all, and it was built with old technology. They grow bananas inside year-round and pay an electric bill of about $5 per month.

Photovoltaic systems could supply a considerable portion of our electricity demand. Photovoltaics only generate electricity during the day, but that is when demand peaks. And utility grids can incorporate intermittent sources as long as they are not more than about 30 percent of the total.

The costs of solar electricity have come down drastically in recent years, even though federal research and development funds have virtually dried up since the Reagan administration. Solar energy plants have had their problems in recent years, especially from losing research and development money, tax breaks, and long-term contracts that were needed to attract investors. But now major energy companies are becoming interested; BP Amoco and Shell are investing seriously in photovoltaics. As pressure to reduce greenhouse gases increases, others will likely get involved as well. There is, in other words, not only a vast potential but also a realistic future for solar energy.

Wind and Biomass Energy

Wind is another renewable source. In the 1970s a lot of research was done to discover the best designs for windmills to generate electricity. Utility regulations, especially in California, encouraged this development and costs came down rapidly. But, as in the case of solar electricity, the tax breaks and long-term commitments needed for further development and economies of scale disappeared. Today, the initiative for developing wind power has shifted to Europe, where Denmark especially has taken the lead. The Danes already generate 8 percent of their electricity from wind. The European Union plans to generate 10 percent of its electricity from wind by the year 2030.

Wind power is now the fastest-growing electricity sector, increasing by over 25 percent per year through the 1990s. And wind power is once again increasing in the United States. Its potential for protecting climate is demonstrated by Tom Gray of the American Wind Energy Association: "In the 12 months ended June 30 [1999] more than 1,000 megawatts of wind equipment were installed in the U.S., enough to serve more than a quarter of a million households and reduce emissions of air pollutants by more than 50 tons a day. It's also enough to cut emissions of carbon dioxide, the leading greenhouse gas, by 6,000 tons daily. To get the same CO_2 reduction benefit by cutting auto use, we would have to take roughly 250,000 sport utility vehicles (or 800,000 fuel-efficient cars) off the roads."

A third renewable is biomass, typically the use of plant material as fuel to produce power. Burning biomass releases CO_2, of course, but the farms or plantations where the trees or other plants are grown would be replanted, and the new growth would take up the CO_2. The use of biomass thus does not add to the total of greenhouse gases and the fossil fuels that it replaces stay in the ground, safely storing their carbon.

As already noted, planting trees can take up and store a lot of carbon, offsetting much of our greenhouse gas emissions. Where the land is not very productive, it is best to plant trees and let the new forests mature and store the carbon. But on productive land, the best greenhouse policy is to harvest the trees for fuel and then replant. This has the added advantage of providing income from a crop for the owners of the land. In the United States, according to [Lynn] Wright and [Evan] Hughes, the best option would be to use some 100 million acres of cropped bottomlands that are marginal for grain crops but would be suitable for tree plantations.

Electricity from biomass is already a commercial technology. Sweden gets 14 percent of its energy from biomass and plans to increase this substantially. In the United States, the paper and pulp industry gets power from burning the waste generated by its production processes.

Another type of biomass is cellulosic ethanol. Ethanol can be made from waste materials produced by agriculture and forest products industries or from energy crops grown for the purpose of fuel production. Ethanol could displace 10–15 percent of our gasoline immediately, since cars sold in America today can burn gasohol. With modifications, cars can burn fuels with higher proportions of ethanol, and even ethanol straight.

As a final example—and this is by no means meant to be

a complete list of all possible renewable energy sources—the future may belong to hydrogen. Hydrogen can be burned as a gas, producing water and no greenhouse gases at all, but storage and transportation would require a completely new infrastructure.

The Benefits of Fuel Cells

The technology currently receiving the most attention, however, is the fuel cell. A fuel cell works like electrolysis, only in reverse. Instead of passing an electric current through water, producing hydrogen and oxygen, a fuel cell combines hydrogen and oxygen, producing water and electricity.

Fuel cells have long been used for power in the space program. For generating useable amounts of power on earth, fuel cells have been bulky. This would not be a problem for generating electricity for a building, and one scenario for the future is for individual buildings to have their own fuel cell generators. (Fuel cells can also be used in central generating plants.) Size has been a barrier, however, for powering vehicles, but development has been very rapid, with Ford, General Motors, DaimlerChrysler, and others actively involved. There are several buses in Chicago that run on fuel cells, and a fleet of forty-five cars and buses powered by fuel cells will be tested in California in the next four years. Mercedes-Benz has now reduced the size of a fuel cell motor so that it fits into its smallest compact car. Several companies plan to begin selling fuel cell cars by 2004.

Since a fuel cell generates electricity, the vehicle does not need the bulky storage batteries and long recharge time that limited the usefulness of previous electric cars, and its range is comparable to a gasoline-powered car. Storing the hydrogen is a major problem. Rather than keep the gas in a heavy, bulky tank in the vehicle, Mercedes-Benz stores the hydrogen as a liquid. Most projects, however, produce hydrogen on the vehicle by chemically extracting it from something else, such as methanol. Chrysler's system extracts hydrogen from gasoline. These systems do emit some CO_2, but this would still be a major improvement because a fuel cell operates at much higher levels of efficiency than a gasoline-powered internal combustion engine. A gasoline engine uses only 20–22 percent of the energy in its fuel; the Mercedes-Benz fuel cell car uses 36 percent. General Motors now has a prototype in a compact car that operates at between 53 percent and 67 percent efficiency.

This short summary is only meant to indicate the possibilities for reducing CO_2 emissions from generating electricity with fossil fuels and, more importantly, the tremendous potential of renewable energy sources that do not emit greenhouse gases at all (or at least do not add to them). Renewables could supply more than half of the entire world's energy needs by 2050.

The major reason renewable sources of energy have not penetrated the market much beyond token levels is that, even though their costs have come town dramatically, they are still more expensive than energy from fossil fuels. But—and this is the critical point for policy—the only reason fossil fuels are so cheap is that the costs of the externalities they impose on society are not included in their prices. If the prices of fossil fuels included the costs of the damages they cause—as both economic theory and conservative principles say that they should—then renewable energy sources would already be competitive or very close to it.

"A renewable fuel mandate will worsen the environment."

Renewable Energy Is Expensive and Will Not Prevent Pollution

Jerry Taylor

In the following viewpoint Jerry Taylor argues that wind power and other types of renewable energy have significant economic and environmental drawbacks. According to Taylor, renewable energy is at least twice as expensive as gas or coal-fired electricity, with government subsidies unlikely to close the price gap. He also opines that environmentalists are wrong to claim that renewable fuels will help prevent air pollution, contending that the most affordable source of this energy, biomass (plant material), causes more environmental damage than natural gas. Taylor is the director of natural resource studies at the libertarian think tank Cato Institute.

As you read, consider the following questions:
1. According to Taylor, what percentage of electricity is generated by renewable energy (excluding hydropower)?
2. According to a study cited by Taylor, how many cents of environmental damage are created by each kilowatt of energy produced by biomass fuels?
3. What does the author believe the U.S. Senate should do if it wants to promote environmentally friendly energy?

[I n the summer of 2003,] the Senate passed an energy bill that is 5 parts corporate welfare to 1 part Soviet-style central planning. An example of the latter aspect is a provision ordering power companies to get 10 percent of their electricity from renewable fuels. While environmentalists are giddy over it, they should think again—a renewable energy mandate will harm, not help, both the economy and the environment.

The High Costs of Renewable Energy

Here's the basic problem: Renewable energy is simply far more expensive than energy produced from natural gas or coal. If it were otherwise, government would not have to contemplate forcing companies to use renewables. How much more expensive? Well, it depends on the specific fuel and the particular facility, but the cheapest sources of renewable energy—biomass (wood, plant fiber, and the like) and wind—cost almost twice as much on average as gas or coal-fired electricity.

Even the blizzard of federal and state tax subsidies and preferences already showered on renewable fuels—subsidies that, on average, reduce costs about 50 percent—have been unable to close the gap. If we take hydropower out of the mix, renewable energy generates about 2.2 percent of the electricity humming along the national grid. Wind power—the darling of the left—generates all of 0.13 percent of the electricity on the nation's grid, and solar is responsible for only 0.02 percent.

While proponents of renewable energy blame subsidies for competing fuels for their tiny market share, the charge falls flat. After studying the matter, the U.S. General Accounting Office found that fossil fuel subsidies are "too small to have a significant effect on the overall level of energy prices and consumption in the United States."

What about this exponential increase in renewable energy, particularly wind power, we keep hearing about? Well, it doesn't take much to show huge increases in market share when current production is so infinitesimal. But the main reason for the growth in renewables isn't improving economics, it's increasingly bossy politicians. Of the 5,356 megawatts of renewable energy production currently on the drawing board, only 291 megawatts would be generated voluntarily. The remainder is being built because state legislators have ordered it to be built.

Capital Costs for Various Electricity-Generating Technologies	
Technology	Capital Costs per Installed Kilowatt
Gas/oil combined cycle	$445
Advanced gas/oil combined cycle	$576
Wind	$983
Coal	$1,092
Coal gasification cycle	$1,306
Waste and landfill gas combustion	$1,395
Geothermal	$1,708
Biomass	$1,732
Fuel cells	$2,041
Advanced nuclear	$2,188
Solar thermal	$2,946
Solar photovoltaic	$4,252

Energy Information Administration, "Assumptions to the Annual Energy Outlook, 2001," December 2000.

Tired of piling subsidy upon subsidy with still nothing to show for it, the Senate takes the states' "build-it-or-else" approach nationwide by requiring power companies to use renewable energy for 10 percent of their electricity by 2020. Proponents argue (correctly) that these production orders would only increase the price of power by a few percentage points—so why not put the pedal to the metal?

Significant Environmental Damage

If the prospect of larger electricity bills isn't a good enough reason to oppose this form of corporate welfare, how about the virtual guarantee that these provisions would worsen environmental quality?

The root of the problem: The cheapest form of renewable energy today is biomass. The Energy Information Administration (a respected analytic arm of the Energy Department) projects about 80 percent of the renewable energy produced to comply with a 10 percent renewable energy mandate would come from biomass fed into existing coal plants.

A recent comprehensive review of the literature undertaken by Thomas Sundqvist and Patrik Soderholm in the *Journal of Energy Literature* suggests the scope of the possible environmental damage. The median finding of 22 separate studies concerning the environmental effect of biomass fuels is that they impose about 7 cents of environmental damage for every kilowatt of energy produced—much greater than the environmental damage caused by nuclear power (about 4 cents), about the same as the environmental damage caused by natural gas–fired electricity, and only slightly less than the environmental damage caused by coal-fired electricity (about 9 cents).

Accordingly, a renewable fuel mandate will worsen the environment because biomass co-fired with coal is clearly more environmentally problematic than is natural gas, the fuel that is currently attracting about 98 percent of the investment dollars for new electricity generation and the fuel most likely to be displaced by a federally imposed renewable energy mandate.

If the Senate were serious about promoting environmentally friendly energy technologies, it would simply impose a tax to reflect the unpriced environmental damages done by various fuels and leave decisions to the marketplace thereafter. But simply ordering the electricity sector around as if the Senate were the Politburo and private utilities were arms of the state will benefit neither the economy nor the environment.

*"Recycling is designed to ease the impact we
have on our environments."*

Recycling Can Reduce Pollution

Sam Martin

The production of paper and plastic releases toxic chemicals
that pollute the air and destroy the ozone layer. In the following viewpoint Sam Martin argues that recycling programs can help decrease pollution and waste by enabling
these products to be reused and turned into clothes and
other items. He further contends that people widely support
mandatory recycling programs. Martin is a writer for *Mother
Earth News*, a magazine about sustainable living.

As you read, consider the following questions:
1. What is Martin's main criticism of landfills?
2. According to the National Recycling Coalition, what
   percentage of the U.S. population has access to a
   recycling facility?
3. According to the author, why has the recycling industry
   not received adequate financial support?

To understand the national obsession with saving our garbage we have only to look to the pages of the *Seguin Gazette*, a newspaper in South Texas. "Nothing is junk—save all scrap metal so it can be recycled," a reporter urges. "In multicar families use only one car . . . and take up walking. [Do] your grocery shopping twice a week instead of every day, and if you live close to the market area walk and take your own basket." The story would read like a how-to brochure on environmentally sustainable living in the 21st century—if it weren't an announcement for the War Effort, circa 1942.

During World War II the fact that saving empty toothpaste tubes would keep the country's water and air clean wasn't of imminent concern. Recycling for the war was simple: Save now, have a better world to live in later. Sixty years later, has the message changed so much?

Recognizing America's Waste Problem

It's no secret that the United States is the most wasteful country on the planet. We dispose of 210 million tons of municipal waste every year, and the yearly costs of that disposal is just shy of $45 billion. Combine residential and business garbage with the truckloads of industrial waste produced in the U.S. and we have an annual pile of trash weighing 12 billion tons. Not surprisingly, what we do with our detritus has become a war of its own.

America's most recent wake-up call to the mess it was making came in 1987, when a trash barge called the Mobro 4000 motored up and down the Eastern seaboard looking for a landfill in which to dump 3,200 tons of New York State's garbage. During thousands of miles of fruitless wandering (the Mobro eventually returned to port, still fully loaded), trash became a headline attraction in newspapers and television stations all over the country.

While waste was news, each story prompted more and more people to question the ethics behind throwing away so much at one time. In 1988, the Environmental Protection Agency (EPA) took the issue seriously enough to recommend that 25% of municipal trash be recycled by the end of a five-year program.

Twelve years of good effort, endless debates and considerable expense have actually made a difference. As of 1995 27% of the country's waste was recycled (compared to 6.3% in 1960), and projected numbers for 2001 report Americans reusing 30% to 35% with recovery rates for paper exceeding 45%.

Nonetheless, what does recycling do for us on a day-to-day basis? It certainly keeps us busy. We set up elaborate sorting systems in our homes—with glass in one bin and paper in the next, rinsing here and bundling there upon penalty of fines or worse: missing the pickup date! And what about the fact that recycling itself is a dirty business, with loud collection trucks plying the predawn streets? It's expensive, as is normal waste disposal, and in increasingly mandatory fashion our taxes are used to pay for an industry that struggles to turn a profit. Is recycling worth it?

Dr. Alan Hershkowitz, director of the National Resources Defense Council, thinks it is. "Everything costs money," he cautions, "including incinerators and landfills." The difference, he explains, is that recycling is designed to ease the impact we have on our environments and alleviate the burden our waste has on our communities. "So yes," Hershkowitz says, "it is worth it."

Since tax money is at the root of any waste solution, the question remains: How can we use the money to deal with our waste most effectively, decrease risks to human health, and foster a healthy environment to live in? It seems that, compared to landfilling, recycling is the economic and environmental favorite by a long shot.

Landfills Versus Recycling

If done right, landfills can be a viable disposal option. If done wrong, they can be an environmental and economic disaster.

The main problem with landfills is that they are complicated structures that are difficult to maintain. Of particular concern is the wastewater created inside landfills as leachate. In order to keep the toxic material from leaking into the local drinking water, these football stadium–sized holes require a combination of liners made from clay, high-density polyethylene (HDPE) plastic or composite membranes. But according to the Environmental Research Foundation in Annapolis, Maryland, clay will dry and crack over time, HDPE will degrade with household chemicals, and composite liners made from clay and plastic will leak somewhere between 0.2 and 10 gallons a day after ten years. Even with complex leachate collection plumbing built into landfills, none of these solutions is 100% foolproof (collection pipes tend to clog and back up).

Superior to Trash Disposal

[A study] performed by Franklin Associates indicates that curbside recycling programs reduce energy use and many kinds of air and water pollution. In no respect was ordinary trash disposal deemed environmentally superior. According to the report, a typical curbside recycling program that collects steel and aluminum containers, newspapers, glass, and certain kinds of plastic will eliminate, for every ton of waste processed, 620 pounds of carbon dioxide, 30 pounds of methane, 5 pounds of carbon monoxide, 2.5 pounds of particulate matter (soot and ash), and varying amounts of other pollutants. The greatest benefits come from replacing virgin raw materials such as wood and petroleum in manufacturing processes with recycled materials. It takes less than 25 percent as much energy to make aluminum cans from recycled cans as from virgin ore, for instance.

Michael Brower and Warren Leon, *The Consumer's Guide to Effective Environmental Choices*, 1999.

"The EPA technicians that currently oversee landfill design and regulation have said that their own engineering standards would not last," warns Will Ferretti, executive director of the National Recycling Coalition. "They're saying that they could break down in a 30-year time frame. It's clearly a concern and we have asked the EPA to revisit their regulations in that light."

To be fair, however, recycling doesn't clear every environmental hurdle either. Products remade from recycled waste such as paper and plastic go through a chemical process. In the case of newsprint, there are a dozen or so supposedly nonhazardous chemicals used in the remanufacturing process, including a water/hydrogen peroxide solution to remove ink from the used paper. Paper recycling also uses thousands of gallons of water.

Compared to making paper from virgin materials, however, recycling is clearly more responsible to the environment. In addition to the hundreds of highly toxic chemicals used in papermaking such as chlorine, dioxin and furan, consider what it takes to harvest a forest, build logging roads, and cut and haul trees. The paper recycling industry alone saves 17 trees for every ton of paper it keeps out of the landfill. In 1996 America recovered 42.3 million tons of paper, saving more than 719 million trees.

The plastic manufacturing industry provides an even more compelling case for re-use. According to Hershkowitz, the production of plastics from crude petroleum causes "some of the most substantial public health threats" of any manufacturing process. Indeed, in 1994 U.S. plastic production was responsible for 111 million pounds of toxic air emissions and 12 million pounds of ozone-depleting chemicals.

"You have to ask which activity leaves a smaller footprint on the environment," says Ferretti when comparing recycling to landfilling. "Recycling relies on industrial activity to function, and industrial activity, by nature, has byproducts that can affect the environment. But from a life cycle standpoint, recycling is much more preferable [to landfills] because it has the least impact."

Consequently, the amount of landfills in the U.S. has decreased from 8,000 in 1988 to just over 3,000 in 1996.

An Economical Idea

The "reuse and recycle" solution is not a new idea; it has, however, long been recognized as the most economically savvy one. Corporations and big industry such as Ford Motor Co., Herman Miller Furniture and Interface Carpets have been doing it for years because they save millions of dollars by cutting back on production costs. If the numbers don't prove recycling's worth, then common sense does.

"Certainly there is a segment of the population that believes that they have a God-given right to just use stuff up and throw it away," offers Ferretti. "But I don't think that segment of the population will always exist."

The statistics overwhelmingly support his prediction. The most recent EPA statistics (1997) reported that curbside pickup was available in over 49 states and 8,000 cities (Hawaii has since joined the team), and the National Recycling Coalition has estimated that around 84% of the population now has access to a recycling facility. As a result, the amount of municipal waste that has been recycled in the last decade has nearly doubled. By all accounts—public opinion polls and government studies included—people seem to want to recycle.

Of course, they also have to recycle. Fines and penalties for ignoring recycling laws are stiff, and this Big Brother finger-wagging is part of what prompted John Tierney, a *New York Times* reporter, to write his scathing rebuttal of the whole philosophy in 1996. Entitled "Recycling is Garbage," Tierney's article asserts that the resources, labor and sum personal time involved in recycling far outweigh any environmental or economic benefit. He further suggests that we not only have plenty of landfill space, but that landfills are an economic boon to the communities surrounding them. Tierney's engaging style was an instant hit among anti-recycling political activists, but his often curious interpretation of facts left many scientists puzzled.

"Nothing is perfectly efficient," says Hershkowitz, "and no one I know of is seriously suggesting 100% recovery for recycling. Still, the main roadblock to increased levels of recycling is the absence of a commitment to this issue by industries that have many economic incentives not to recycle or use recycled materials."

Increasing Consumer Support

Which brings us to a problem in the recycling industry: consumer support. Widely considered the weakest link in the recycling loop, recycled product sales are not what they should be—either because recycled products are more expensive or because they're unavailable. For that reason, the recycling industry isn't getting the financial support it needs to compete with the federally subsidized incentives to which Hershkowitz refers. Most people simply don't realize that they have the option to buy recycled.

"Aluminum, steel and glass are under our noses, and they're not marked like paper usually is," explains George Rutherford of America Recycles Day. "But aluminum, steel and glass have a 30% to 40% recycled content. Plastic doesn't. It's by and large a virgin product. Also, cars are one of the most widely recycled products we have."

Nevertheless, the enormous enthusiasm for recycling programs suggests that there are plenty of reasons to recycle other than being able to buy more stuff, remanufactured or not.

"Recycling is one of those few activities that [allow us] to make a direct connection between our behaviors and some kind of contribution to a quality of life that is hard to find out there," explains Ferretti. "Maybe altruistic is the right word, but I think there's something more innate and more satisfying that is occurring. I would argue that the quality of life both now and for your children and grandchildren is enhanced by that rather modest and mundane action of separating out some portion of our waste and putting it out at the curb for recycling."

While human nature is oftentimes up for speculation, the fact that recycling is the best solution for waste disposal isn't. The evidence and the desire have never been more telling.

Millions of Pounds of Waste

Americans receive almost 4 million tons of junk mail a year—44% is never opened.

Every day, U.S. businesses generate enough paper to circle the earth 20 times. In 1960, Americans disposed of 2.7 pounds of waste per person per day. By 1990, the number had risen to 4.3 pounds per person per day. Every ton of paper recycled saves approximately 17 trees.

Americans throw away 2.5 million plastic bottles every hour.

Five recycled soft drink bottles will make enough fiberfill for a man's ski jacket. 1,050 recycled milk jugs can be made into a six-foot park bench. The United States makes enough plastic film each year to shrink-wrap the state of Texas. If only 10% of Americans bought products with less plastic packaging only 10% of the time, approximately 144 million pounds of plastic could be eliminated from our landfills.

Styrofoam is nonrecyclable. Each year Americans throw away 25 billion Styrofoam cups.

Five hundred years from now, the foam coffee cup you used this morning will be sitting in a landfill. If all morning newspapers read around the country were recycled, 41,000 trees would be saved daily and 6 million tons of waste would never end up in landfills.

"Recycling is a manufacturing process, and therefore it too has environmental impact."

Recycling Does Not Reduce Pollution

Daniel Benjamin

In the following viewpoint Daniel Benjamin maintains that mandatory curbside recycling is unnecessary and does not prevent pollution. He argues that despite the claims of environmental groups and the beliefs of millions of Americans, the United States has plenty of room for its garbage. Benjamin contends that recycling is not only unnecessary but that curbside recycling actually increases air pollution and wastes resources by requiring more garbage trucks to travel residential neighborhoods. Benjamin is an economics professor at Clemson University and a senior researcher at the Property and Environment Research Center (PERC), an organization that advocates free-market solutions to environmental problems.

As you read, consider the following questions:

1. When did the modern era of recycling begin, according to Benjamin?
2. In the author's opinion, when does the loss of forest land occur?
3. According to the author, how much more expensive is curbside recycling in comparison to disposal?

Daniel Benjamin, "The Eight Myths of Recycling," *American Enterprise*, vol. 15, January/February 2004, p. 52. Copyright © 2004 by the American Enterprise Institute for Public Policy Research. Reproduced by permission of *The American Enterprise*, a magazine of Politics, Business, and Culture. On the Web at www. TAEmag.com.

Garbage is the unavoidable by-product of production and consumption. There are three ways to deal with it, all known and used since antiquity: dumping, burning, and recycling. For thousands of years it was commonplace to dump rubbish on site—on the floor, or out the window. Scavenging domestic animals, chiefly pigs and dogs, consumed the edible parts, and poor people salvaged what they could. The rest was covered and built upon.

Eventually, humans began to use more elaborate methods of dealing with their rubbish. The first modern incinerator (called a "destructor") went into operation in Nottingham, England in 1874. After World War II, landfills became the accepted means of dealing with trash. The modern era of the recycling craze can be traced to 1987, when the garbage barge Mobro 4000 had to spend two months touring the Atlantic and the Gulf of Mexico before it found a home for its load. The Environmental Defense Fund, the National Solid Waste Management Association (whose members were anxious to line up new customers for their expanding landfill capacity), the press, and finally the Enviromnental Protection Agency, spun the story of a garbage crisis out of control. By 1995, the majority of Americans thought trash was our number one environmental problem—with 77 percent reporting that increased recycling of household rubbish was the solution. Yet these claims and fears were based on errors and misinformation, which I have compiled into the Eight Great Myths of Recycling.

Myth 1: Our Garbage Will Bury Us

Fact: Even though the United States is larger, more affluent, and producing more garbage, it now has more landfill capacity than ever before. The erroneous opposite impression comes from old studies that counted the number of landfills (which has declined) rather than landfill capacity (which has grown). There are a few places, like New Jersey, where capacity has shrunk. But the uneven distribution of landfill space is no more important than the uneven distribution of automobile manufacturing. Perhaps the most important fact is this: If we permitted our rubbish to grow to the height of New York City's famous Fresh Kills landfill (225 feet), a site only about 10 miles on a side could hold all of America's garbage for the next century.

Myth 2: Our Garbage Will Poison Us

Fact: Almost anything can pose a theoretical threat, but evidence of actual harm from landfills is almost non-existent, as the Environmental Protection Agency itself acknowledges. The EPA has concluded that landfills constructed according to agency regulations can be expected to cause a total of 5.7 cancer-related deaths over the next 300 years. It isn't household waste, but improperly or illegally dumped industrial wastes that can be harmful. Household recycling programs have no effect on those wastes, a fact ignored by messianic proponents of recycling.

Myth 3: Our Packaging Is Immoral

Fact: Many people argue that the best way to "save landfill space" is to reduce the amount of packaging Americans use, via mandatory controls. But packaging can actually reduce total garbage produced and total resources used. The average American family generates fully one third less trash than does the average Mexican household. The reason is that our intensive use of packaging yields less spoilage and breakage, thereby saving resources, and producing, on balance, less total rubbish. Careful packaging also reduces food poisoning and other health problems.

Over the past 25 years, market incentives have already reduced the weights of individual packages by 30 to 70 percent. An average aluminum can weighed nearly 21 grams in 1972; in 2002, that same can weighs in at under 14 grams. A plastic grocery sack was 2.3 mils thick in 1976; by 2001, it was a mere 0.7 mils.

By contrast, the environmentally sensitive *New York Times* has been growing. A year's worth of the newspaper now weighs 520 pounds and occupies more than 40 cubic feet in a landfill. This is equivalent in weight to 17,180 aluminum cans—nearly a century's worth of beer and soft drink consumption by one person. Clearly, people anxious to heal Mother Earth must forego the *Times*!

Myth 4: We Must Achieve "Trash Independence"

Fact: Garbage has become an interstate business, with 47 states exporting the stuff and 45 importing it. Environmentalists contend that each state should dispose within its borders all the trash produced within its borders. But why? Transporting garbage across an arbitrary legal boundary has no effect on the environmental impact of the disposal of that material. Moving a ton of trash is no more hazardous than moving a ton of any other commodity.

Myth 5: We Are Squandering Irreplaceable Resources

Fact: Thanks to numerous innovations, we now produce about twice as much output per unit of energy as we did 50 years ago, and five times as much as we did 200 years ago. Automobiles use only half as much metal as in 1970, and one optical fiber carries the same number of calls as 625 copper wires did 20 years ago. Bridges are built with less steel, because steel is stronger and engineering is improved. Automobile and truck engines consume less fuel per unit of work performed, and produce fewer emissions.

To address the issue of paper, the most-promoted form of

recycling: The amount of new growth that occurs each year in forests is more than 20 times the number of trees consumed by the world each year for wood and paper. Where loss of forest land is taking place, as in tropical rain forests, it can be traced directly to a lack of private property rights. Governments have used forests, especially the valuable tropical ones, as an easy way to raise quick cash.

Wherever private property rights to forests are well-defined and enforced, forests are either stable or growing. More recycling of paper or cardboard would not eliminate tropical forest losses.

Myth 6: Recycling Always Protects the Environment

Fact: Recycling is a manufacturing process, and therefore it too has environmental impact. The U.S. Office of Technology Assessment says that it is "not clear whether secondary manufacturing [i.e., recycling] produces less pollution per ton of material processed than primary manufacturing." Recycling merely changes the nature of pollution—sometimes decreasing it, and sometimes increasing it.

This effect is particularly apparent in the case of curbside recycling, which is mandated or strongly encouraged by governments in many communities around the country. Curbside recycling requires that more trucks be used to collect the same amount of waste materials. Instead of one truck picking up 40 pounds of garbage, one will pick up four pounds of recyclables and a second will collect 36 pounds of rubbish.

Los Angeles has estimated that due to curbside recycling, its fleet of trucks is twice as large as it otherwise would be— 800 vs. 400 trucks. This means more iron ore and coal mining, more steel and rubber manufacturing, more petroleum extracted and refined for fuel—and of course all that extra air pollution in the Los Angeles basin as the 400 added trucks cruise the streets.

Myth 7: Recycling Saves Resources

Fact: Using less of one resource usually means using more of another. Curbside recycling is substantially more costly and uses far more resources than a program in which disposal is combined with a voluntary drop-off/buy-back option. The reason: Curbside recycling of household rubbish uses huge amounts of capital and labor per pound of material recycled. Overall, curbside recycling costs between 35 and 55 percent more than simply disposing of the item. It typically wastes resources.

In the ordinary course of daily living, we already reuse most higher value items. The only things that intentionally end up in the trash are both low in value and costly to reuse or recycle. Yet these are the items that municipal recycling programs are targeting—the very things that consumers have already decided are too worthless or costly to deal with further. All of the profitable, socially productive opportunities for recycling were long ago co-opted by the private sector, because they pay back. The bulk of all curbside recycling programs simply wastes resources.

Myth 8: Without Forced Mandates, There Would Not Be Any Recycling

Fact: Long before state or local governments had even contemplated the word recycling, the makers of steel, aluminum, and thousands of other products were recycling manufacturing scraps. Some operated post-consumer drop-off centers.

As for the claim that the private sector promotes premature or excessive disposal, this ignores an enormous body of evidence to the contrary. Firms only survive in the marketplace if they take into account all costs. Fifty years ago, when labor was cheap compared to materials, goods were built to be repaired, so that the expensive materials could be used for a longer period of time. As the price of labor has risen and the cost of materials has fallen, manufacturers have responded by building items to be used until they break, and then discarded. There is no bias against recycling; there is merely a market-driven effort to conserve the most valuable resources.

Informed, voluntary recycling conserves resources and raises our wealth, enabling us to achieve valued ends that would otherwise be impossible. Mandatory programs, however, in which people are directly or indirectly compelled to do what they know is not sensible, routinely make society worse off. Such programs force people to squander valuable resources in a quixotic quest to save what they would sensibly discard.

Except in a few rare cases, the free market is eminently capable of providing both disposal and recycling in an amount and mix that creates the greatest wealth for society. This makes possible the widest and most satisfying range of human endeavors. Simply put, market prices are sufficient to induce the trash-man to come, and to make his burden bearable, and neither he nor we can hope for any better than that.

Periodical Bibliography

The following articles have been selected to supplement the diverse views presented in this chapter.

Mary H. Cooper	"Water Quality," *CQ Researcher*, November 24, 2000.
Richard A. Halpern	"1491 and All That," *American Outlook*, November/December 2000.
David Hochschild and Arlie Hochschild	"Hooray for the Red, White, Blue, and Green," *Los Angeles Times*, November 11, 2001.
Albert L. Huebner	"The Cost of Fossil Fuels," *Humanist*, March/April 2003.
Issues and Controversies On File	"Air Pollution," March 26, 1999.
Angela Logomasini	"Forced Recycling Is a Waste," *Wall Street Journal*, March 19, 2002.
Jim Motavalli	"End Tailpipe Tyranny," *New Internationalist*, June 2003.
Jim Motavalli	"Zero Waste," *E: The Environmental Magazine*, March 2001.
Joseph Orlins and Anne Wehrly	"The Quest for Clean Water," *World & I*, May 2003.
Michael Renner	"Going to Work for Wind Power," *World Watch*, January/February 2001.
R.W. Rushing	"Greener than Thou," *Whole Earth*, Summer 2001.
Payal Sampat	"The Hidden Threat of Groundwater Pollution," *USA Today Magazine*, July 2001.
Lynn Scarlett	"'Green Guilt' Only Makes Things Worse," *Los Angeles Times*, July 8, 1999.
Roddy Scheer	"Parks as Lungs," *E: The Environmental Magazine*, November/December 2001.
David G. Streets	"Policy and Technology for Clean Air," *Forum for Applied Research and Public Policy*, Winter 1999.

CHAPTER 3

Is the American Lifestyle Bad for the Environment?

Chapter Preface

Many people around the world have claimed that the American lifestyle harms the environment. One area of criticism is Americans' eating habits. The average American household consumes a total of nine pounds of beef, pork, lamb, chicken, and turkey each week. As a result of concerns about how this consumption affects the environment, many people have elected to follow vegetarian diets. Advocates of vegetarianism assert that avoiding animal products is wise because the raising of livestock and poultry seriously damages the environment. They contend that more Americans should adopt a vegetarian lifestyle in order to help preserve the nation's resources.

Supporters of vegetarian diets claim there are several ways the meat and poultry industry harms land. In his book *The Greening of Conservative America*, John R.E. Bliese explains that because cows stay in one place when they graze, unlike nomadic animals like elk or bison, they gradually turn those areas into wastelands. Bliese further notes, "In many arid places the land is covered with fragile cryptogamic crusts . . . [that] are critical for protecting the soil from erosion and for fixing nitrogen in these ecosystems. Cattle trample and destroy these crusts, severely reducing the productivity of the land." Land that is used and destroyed in the raising of livestock could be better utilized for farming, assert vegetarians. For example, the British organization Vegfam claims that a ten-acre farm that supports two cows could instead be used to support sixty people who are growing soybeans or two dozen people who are growing wheat.

Vegetarians also contend that meat-based diets cause pollution and use up significant amounts of water. The waste produced by animals can cause water pollution, while the methane gas emitted by cows has been linked to global warming. Environmental writer Jim Motavalli asserts, "Energy-intensive U.S. factory farms generated 1.4 billion tons of animal waste in 1996, which, the Environmental Protection Agency reports, pollutes American waterways more than all other industrial sources combined." The pesticides and fertilizers needed to grow the massive amounts of grain consumed by livestock and poultry also results in water pollution. In addition, vegetarians contend that meat eating wastes water. Motavalli claims that more water is used in the United States to produce beef than is required to grow all of the nation's fruits and vegetables.

Polls have shown that approximately 2.5 percent of Americans are vegetarians, while many others have cut back on meat and poultry consumption. Many of these people believe their lifestyle has a less severe impact on the environment than the lifestyle of most Americans. In the following chapter the authors examine the effects that the typical American has on the nation's resources.

"The average North American lifestyle requires almost 10 acres of ecologically productive lands to supply its resources."

American Consumption Patterns Destroy the Environment

David Schaller

In the following viewpoint David Schaller maintains that the consumption patterns of Americans and citizens of other developed nations are harmful to the environment. According to Schaller, Americans use more natural resources and create more waste than do people living in developing countries. He concludes that the development of environmental policies must take these disproportionate patterns into account. Schaller is a sustainable development expert with the Denver regional office of the Environmental Protection Agency.

As you read, consider the following questions:
1. What is an ecological footprint, as explained by Schaller?
2. According to the author, by what factor do the ecological requirements of citizens in wealthy nations exceed the "global per capita supply of resources"?
3. By which methods have Americans "appropriated" ecological resources outside this nation's borders, in Schaller's view?

David Schaller, "Our Footprints Are All over the Place," *Regulatory Intelligence Data*, February 5, 1999.

The word "footprint" offers us many richly symbolic images: Neil Armstrong's "one small step"; [Robinson] Crusoe's Friday; [Carl] Sandburg's fog that comes "on little cat feet"; the [fossilized] Olduvai tracks of Australopithecus; and yes, even the caution expressed by my elementary school teacher to stay away from "Big Feet"—the junior high kids on the playground who loved to torment first- and second-graders.

Let's consider another type of footprint, one equally symbolic and full of meaning to those concerned about environmental protection.

If asked who had the bigger "footprint"—an adult female living somewhere in the developing world or your average eight-year-old American child—most would select the adult female. Now, insert the word "ecological" in front of "footprint" and repeat the question. The answer may surprise.

Ecological Footprints

The concept of an "ecological footprint" turns out to be an almost intuitive measure of the impact of individuals or societies on nature. It provides a simple yet elegant accounting tool that can help us see the impact of human consumption patterns on the earth. What we do about this information, of course, is the essence of a much larger policy debate.

As we live out our lives, we consume resources and discard wastes. Each bit of consumption and generation of waste demands a certain amount of productive land and water. The amount of productive land and water needed to support the production of resources we consume and absorb the wastes we create can be considered our ecological footprint.

Individuals, households, cities, regions, nations—all can be measured as to their ecological footprint.

In their compelling book, *Our Ecological Footprint*, William Rees and Mathis Wackernagel lay out the approach that is changing the way many look at broad issues of sustainability, ecological carrying capacity, environmental protection, and even social justice. The authors take us through the number crunching and data sources used to calculate footprints for us, our cities, and our nations. For Western societies, the findings are less than comforting.

Resource Inequality

Here, in a nutshell, is "footprint" analysis applied to the world in which we live:

The ecologically productive land of the world now totals some 3.6 acres for each of the 5.9 billion people [alive in 1999]. The average North American lifestyle requires almost 10 acres of ecologically productive lands to supply its resources and absorb its wastes. Thus, the ecological demands of average citizens in wealthy countries exceed global per capita supply of resources by a factor of nearly three. Someone, lots of someones, somewhere are going without.

How Food Affects the Environment

	Global Warming	Air Pollution		Water Pollution		Habitat Alteration	
	Greenhouse Gases	Common	Toxic	Common	Toxic	Water Use	Land Use
Cultivation	4%	52%	39%	73%	17%	99%	82%
Food processing	16	6	1	4	8	0	1
Packaging	8	4	9	5	11	0	9
Transportation	26	15	19	0	0	0	7
Retail	1	1	5	1	0	0	1
Other	46	22	26	17	63	1	1
Total for fruit, vegetables, & grains	100%	100%	100%	100%	100%	100%	100%
As fraction of all impacts	2%	5%	3%	3%	5%	30%	6%

Michael Brower and Warren Leon, *The Consumer's Guide to Effective Environmental Choices*, 1999.

Said another way, if everyone currently alive were to consume resources and generate wastes at the pace of the average citizen in the U.S. (or Canada, or western Europe, or Japan) we would need three planets of ecologically productive lands.

This projection assumes that there will be no improvements in either resource use efficiency or waste elimination techniques. However, we know that improvements in both are happening. The big question is whether they are happening fast enough.

It is, of course, in the inefficiency of resource production that wastes are created, our "environmental" problems manifested, and the Environmental Protection Agency's mission defined. But if we are not looking hard at how and where our "footprint" is placed, we are missing the chance to do something about those inefficiencies.

When we use the ecological footprint concept to measure the resource use and waste generation of the average North American, it becomes clear that via trade and technology we have "appropriated" the ecological capacity of large areas outside our own national boundaries. We have, in fact, exported much of our "footprint." Responsibility for a good deal of the world's environmental problems starts to hit home.

Dealing with the Root Causes

So where do we go with this? Some would prefer to start with that hypothetical adult female in the developing world whose fecundity promises to add billions more footprints to the earth's surface in the coming decades. The accounting tool of ecological footprints suggests, however, that the place to begin is with the resource consuming, waste generating "average" inhabitant of North America, western Europe, and Japan.

Limiting the number of poor people in distant countries may make for popular policy, but it does little about the root cause of our environmental and related socio-economic problems. The two ounces of rice that a billion of our poorest neighbors call their "daily bread" leaves a rather transparent ecological footprint. Those one billion could "go away" tomorrow, and our global ecological unraveling would go on unabated.

The answer to our earlier question? It is the eight-year-old child (not to mention his parents, neighbors, and friends) who now has the "Big Feet."

| *"Consumerism . . . promotes technologies that serve to better environmental and human well-being."*

American Consumption Patterns Are Good for the Environment

Ezra Finkle

Efforts by the United Nations and anticonsumer activist groups to convince Western consumers to reduce consumption ignore the positive effects production and consumption have on the environment, Ezra Finkle argues in the following viewpoint. He argues that consumption spurs the creation of technologies that help developed nations grow food and get rid of waste in environmentally friendly ways. Finkle asserts that policies that aim to reduce consumption are misguided and unfairly blame American consumers for problems facing underdeveloped countries. Finkle is an expert at the Competitive Enterprise Institute, an organization that promotes free market solutions to environmental problems.

As you read, consider the following questions:
1. According to Finkle, what percentage of reforestation in the United States is performed by the private sector?
2. How is DDT invaluable, in the author's view?
3. Why does Finkle believe that the actions of anticonsumer activists are not humanitarian?

Ezra Finkle, "Buy Nothing Day: Sustainable Consumption at the Cost of Sustained Consumption," www.cei.org, December 15, 2003. Copyright © 2003 by the Competitive Enterprise Institute. Reproduced by permission.

"**B**lack Friday." The term evokes images of crowded malls and families rushing to get through Christmas shopping lists. The Friday after Thanksgiving is always one of the busiest shopping days of the year. With Christmas advertising arriving well ahead of Thanksgiving, [2003's] Black Friday was sure to be a big one. But citizens of America's progressive cities, such as San Francisco and Seattle, got more than they bargained for—no pun intended—as protesters also used Black Friday to protest what Adbusters, an anticonsumer activist group, labels a "massive consumption and impulse buying." On November 28, 2003, activists celebrated another "Buy Nothing Day."

Created by a former Canadian advertising consultant [in 1992], "Buy Nothing Day" has grown exponentially via the Web. Adbusters, located in Vancouver, Canada, sees "Buy Nothing Day" as a step toward reexamining the consumption habits of industrialized nations. In a sense, it is a true consumer's holiday—a break from the mayhem ensuing at malls across America every Friday after Thanksgiving.

Simple concept. There are 1001 other places I would rather be than a shopping mall on the Friday after Thanksgiving. However, a closer look beyond the colorful "Buy Nothing Day" festivities of sheep costumes and 'burping corporate pigs' persists the repeated alarmist concern regarding sustainable consumption. An old friend put it best when he said, "Few know the term, but many have heard the lingo." The concept of sustainable consumption, essential to environmental ideologues, surfaces on "Buy Nothing Day." Suddenly, bromides such as Americans are "consuming more quickly than resources could handle" or that "American consumption is pillaging Mother Earth at the expense of the Third World" are heard in progressive cities around the world.

A Flawed UN Agenda

Perhaps by coincidence, the UN held a conference on sustainable consumption at Rio [de Janeiro] in 1992, the same year as Adbusters inaugural "Buy Nothing Day." This meeting of world leaders resulted in Agenda 21, a protocol by which subscribing nations would balance economic development with the efforts to preserve the environment. Written in language broad enough to appeal to groups other than eco-fanatics, Agenda 21 seemed like a good idea.

A closer inspection reveals some flaws that threaten economic growth and individual liberty by promoting misguided international agreements. Principle 8, for example, stipulates, "Nation states should reduce unsustainable patterns of production and consumption and promote appropriate demographic policies." This gives the illusion that nations, especially developed ones, are in dire need of cutting consumption to reach levels that allow for a healthy global environment. Principle 8 and "Buy Nothing Day" advocates promote the idea that Americans are consuming from a dwindling resources pool. Nothing could be further from the truth, however.

Take timber for example. While it is true that the U.S. is the number one timber producer, U.S. forest resources are currently rising. Since 1950, surveys of American forests revealed growth numbers that more than offset harvests. Consumption sends the message to suppliers to produce more forests. Despite the federal government's role as the largest landowner in the United States, approximately 86 percent of the reforestation is done by the private sector. Because of farming and industrial innovations, America now produces more goods on less land and with less labor. Contrary to "Buy Nothing Day" activist statements, American forests are plentiful and growing.

A Dangerous Principle

Regulatory error is also obvious through Principle 15. Principle 15 states: "In order to protect the environment, the precautionary approach shall be widely applied by states according to their capabilities. Where there are threats of irreversible damage, lack of full scientific certainty shall not be used as a reason for postponing cost-effective measures to prevent environmental degradation." This sounds quite similar to the Precautionary Principle. The Precautionary Principle was developed in Germany during the 1970s to initiate a 'look before you leap' approach toward scientific progress.

As sensible as this idea sounds, the Precautionary Principle poses great danger to global welfare and development.

The Precautionary Principle increases regulation through the assumption that all technologies and chemicals are dangerous until proven safe. This statute stands in direct contrast with the trial and error system of development that encourages the "Yankee ingenuity" responsible for America's history of rapid wealth attainment and continuous innovation. The Precautionary Principle seeks zero risk in a world where growth is achieved primarily by risk taking behavior.

Wealth and Cleanliness

Of course the rich consume more than the poor. "Rich" inevitably entails some of that. As it happens, we also produce our abundance far more efficiently than they produce their scarcity, and that makes us richer still. The peasant hunched over his cow-dung fire is not efficient, not green, not living in happy harmony with nature. He is just poor.

And of course the rich generate more waste than the poor. What goes in must come out; productions of goods and garbage rise together, even if the efficiency of our production lines makes our balance more favorable than inefficiency makes theirs. But wealth also lets us handle our waste better. Nobody who knows Calcutta, Mexico City, or tribal Africa could possibly doubt that. The desperately poor live in their own compost heaps and septic systems, and there is nothing green or environmentally harmonious about that.

Peter W. Huber, *Hard Green*, 1999.

The Precautionary Principle further serves as evidence suggesting how sustainable consumption policies are misguided. Under the Precautionary Principle, all cost-effective safety measures are suspended in pursuit of prohibiting the release of substances which might cause harm to the environment or humans even if there persists no proof of connection between technology and harm. This has led to regulatory initiatives that have killed many. Consider the case of DDT [a pesticide]. At the Sustainable Consumption conference in 1992, the United Nations Environment Program's Global Convention on Persistent Organic Pollutants (POPs) banned DDT use. DDT use, however, has proven invaluable in post–World War II efforts in fighting malaria breakouts. Throughout developing nations suffering from malaria, DDT remains their best weapon in preventing this health dilemma from reaching severe levels. "Buy Nothing Day" adherents contradict themselves by parading images of those suffering in the Third World yet maintaining an adversarial position regarding DDT and other advanced pesticides.

Besides DDT, environmental ideologues have long used a Precautionary Principle stance to block biogenetically engineered agriculture. As with DDT, environmental activists lack sufficient data to prove that genetically modified (GM) foods are harmful. Lack of proof, however, has certainly not prevented activists from resorting to preventive action to block genetically modified growth. In 1997, Greenpeace's "Hazard Patrol" blocked a shipment of genetically engineered soya from the U.S. to Brazil. On Adbuster's website, environmental and human rights activists liken genetically modified crops to a harmful class of "Frankenstein foods." Genetically modified farming techniques, however, have proven invaluable in increasing harvest without clearing away more wilderness for agricultural purposes. Again, environmental activists are either misinformed or enforcing a hidden agenda when claiming that agricultural advances through biotechnology will hurt the environment as such advance farming techniques actually increase yields thus preserving more land for wildlife and aesthetic purposes. Human rights activists are also acting foolishly or deviously when they claim that GM foods will exacerbate the woes of those starving in Third World countries. GM techniques enable U.S. producers to send more food aid to developing nations without using as much farmland. GM farming techniques will result in increased incomes for farmers in developing nations while bolstering the available food supply. Unfortunately, activists and some politicians allow the alleged risk of GM foods to eclipse the far greater risk of starving people in technologically underdeveloped nations.

Consumption Is Beneficial

Beyond the festive sheep costumes—aimed at mocking consumers—and dignified "burping pig" contests—used to lambaste corporate America—persists the misguided environmentalist plan for promoting sustainable consumption.

Adbuster activists continue to ignore consumption's benefits. Not only does consumption promote economic stability but, in a free market, leads to resource growth and replenishment. As economist Julian Simon once said "the ultimate resource is people, especially skilled, spirited, hopeful young people who will exert their will and imagination for their own benefit and in doing so, will inevitably benefit the rest of us as well." Rather than contributing to global destruction and Third World poverty, consumerism actually promotes technologies that serve to better environmental and human well-being.

These anti-consumer activists fail to recognize any of the offsetting benefits of consumption. Throughout 2003 Adbusters has been too preoccupied with raising scares about urban sprawl, SUVs, and the credit card culture, ignoring how consumption and demand gave way to cost-effective innovations such as consumer internet access, which, ironically, played a major role in organizing and building the anti-consumer movement. Furthermore, charges against biotechnology and chemical use in developing nations are cruel. Rather than promoting the spread of developed world technologies to Third World countries, anti-consumer activists advocate sustainable consumption via the redistribution of resources from the developed to the Third World. These activists claim to champion the causes of those suffering in the technologically disadvantaged nations, yet they adamantly oppose empowering such nations with the tools required for much needed economic growth. Their actions are not of a humanitarian nature, but rather chauvinistic liberal paternalisms that currently promote sustainable consumption by eliminating all progress made to achieve sustained consumption.

"If the secret to a prosperous economy is producing big useless objects that pollute, then why not produce big useless objects that are benign."

Sport Utility Vehicles Are Bad for the Environment

Albert Koehl

In the following viewpoint Albert Koehl asserts that sport utility vehicles (SUVs) cause significant damage to the environment. He contends that these vehicles emit excessive amounts of carbon dioxide, which contributes to global warming, waste fossil fuel, and are inefficient. Koehl is an environmental lawyer and a former prosecutor with the Ontario Ministry of the Environment.

As you read, consider the following questions:
1. How do SUVs affect children, according to Koehl?
2. How many pounds does the average SUV weigh, as stated by the author?
3. What jobs does Koehl sarcastically suggest are created by the popularity of SUVs?

Albert Koehl, "A Modest Proposal," *Alternatives Journal: Canadian Environmental Ideas and Action*, vol. 29, Spring 2003, p. 52. Copyright © 2003 by *Alternatives*, annual subscriptions (6/yr) $35.00 (plus GST), Faculty of Environmental Studies, University of Waterloo, Waterloo, Ontario N2L 3G1, www.alternativesjournal.ca. Reproduced by permission of the publisher and the author.

Everyone should have a Sub Urban Vanity—or rather a Selfish Upscale Van. Or is it a Simply Unnecessary Vehicle? Forget the name. The ads all say we need one.

The "Advantages" of SUVs

SUVs are ideal for city driving. They are safer, particularly in a collision with someone who doesn't have one.

SUVs make it easier to escape the city. Cities are clogged with noisy cars and trucks spewing toxins, so you need a dependable get-away vehicle. How better to flee than with four-wheel traction, hill descent control and all-terrain, anti-lock brakes?

SUVs give your children a secure environment—an extended warranty cabin where they can drink chilled beverages while they figure out how to cope with the extra carbon dioxide you pump into the atmosphere on their behalf. Why keep fossil fuels in the ground when your kids appreciate a challenge?

Your SUV's seat-cooled three-zone climate-controlled interior provides a comfortable refuge from power-hungry bureaucrats promoting the notion of global warming. Nothing, not even climate chaos, catches you by surprise—you have blind-spot monitoring and the ability to engage in intellectual off-roading.

People without SUVs lack not only fully independent rear suspensions but also imagination. Driving a white SUV, you're no bland commuter—you're an aid worker in Borneo. Get it mud-splattered and you're not putting off the car wash—you're an adventurer on safari chasing down fleeing antelope (wearing bike helmets) in the Valley of the Don. And in Cadillac's new mega-model, with room for eight and cargo, you're not a solo-driving, gas-guzzling boor spewing 15 tonnes of greenhouse gases annually from a vehicle rated a perfect zero by the US EPA [Environmental Protection Agency]—you're a self-sacrificing patriot waiting, for the call to transport troops, arms and bid-suits to the terrorist front.

I used to fret about SUV waste and inefficiency. A big SUV weighs over 6000 pounds, the average driver only about 150. Forty pounds of metal and upholstery to transport a pound of flesh can't make sense, even if you are putting on weight.

Creating a Healthy Economy

If the secret to a prosperous economy is producing big use-less objects that pollute, then why not produce big useless objects that are benign, such as immobile slabs of metal for our driveways. Freed from our cash-eating, gas-gluttons, we might work a day less each week, pool our money for advanced rapid transit and hire a Sherpa clan when we really have to off-road in the Himalayas. There would still be plenty of jobs. Marketing representatives, for instance, could be redeployed from convincing people that Trail Blazers, Pathfinders and Navigators are crucial for finding the corner store, to pitching the envirofriendly slabs as the latest suburban security accessory for homeland defense.

I am no longer so naive. One day, my economic theories so polluted my thoughts while signaling a left from my bike, that I missed the scent of an approaching Durango. A horn blast sent my brain hurtling into my skull's dashboard. A little man leaned out an orifice of the behemoth and bellowed, "Get off the road, you're not a car."

Automobiles Use Up Land

The SUV certainly ranks among the more absurd expressions of American overconsumption (General Motors' Yukon XL Denali, to cite an extreme example, is over 18 feet long and weighs about three tons). But it is too easy to condemn this overgrown behemoth and then hop self-satisfied back into a midsize sedan. Most of what is wrong with the SUV—the resources it swallows, the dangers it poses, and the blight it creates—is wrong with the automobile system as a whole. Automobiles pollute the oceans and the air, over-heat cities and the earth, devour land and time, produce waste and noise, and cause injury and illness.

Here, in more detail, is an indictment of the car as an environmental and public-health menace: . . .

Cars occupy a huge amount of space. Paved roads occupy over 13,000 square miles of land area across the United States—nearly 750 square meters per U.S. motor vehicle—and parking occupies another 3,000 square miles, according to a report by Todd Litman of the Victoria Transport Policy Institute. In urban areas, roads and parking take up 20–30% of the total surface area; in commercial districts, 50–60%.

Alejandro Reuss, *Dollars & Sense*, March/April 2003.

The jolt rearranged my thoughts into a new, lighter order. I realized that I had not been leading the life of an exemplary consumer. I only occasionally bought a cheap tire tube for a flat or demanded emergency services when flattened by a more enlightened SUV driver.

Big SUVs, and smaller vehicles before them, create production jobs and endless spin-off employment. There are maintenance crews for roads, insurance adjusters for the injured, cops and judges for the inebriated, asthma puffer sales reps for kids, grief counsellors for teenagers, and nurses and doctors for the not-quite-roadkill.

The SUV is truly the hemlock-spiced lifeblood of our well-being. The next chapter of this feel-good story is still being written. It will be called: Everyone should have a Hummer.

"SUVs aren't increasing air pollution in cities, and their effect on global warming, if any, is negligible."

Sport Utility Vehicles Do Not Harm the Environment

John Merline

Sport utility vehicles (SUVs) do not pose a danger to the environment, John Merline contends in the following viewpoint. He argues that SUVs do not use significantly more fuel than smaller vehicles and therefore should not be blamed for wasting gasoline. In addition, Merline asserts that environmentalists wrongly claim SUVs contribute to air pollution and global warming; their contribution to these environmental problems is marginal, at best, he claims. Merline is an editorial writer for *USA Today* and a contributing editor for *Consumers' Research Magazine*.

As you read, consider the following questions:
1. What is the miles-per-gallon average of midsize SUVs?
2. According to the Environmental Protection Agency, by what percentage did the amount of nitrogen oxide in the air decrease between 1992 and 2001?
3. In Merline's opinion, why would eliminating all SUVs have little effect on global warming?

John Merline, "Why Customers Have Been Choosing SUVs," *Consumers' Research Magazine*, vol. 86, April 2003, p. 10. Copyright © 2003 by Consumers' Research, Inc. Reproduced by permission.

I n recent months, a variety of consumer groups and environmentalists have launched a ferocious campaign aimed at disarming American drivers of Sport Utility Vehicles (SUVs). One group, the Detroit Project, went so far as to charge that SUV drivers were supporting terrorism every time they filled up their gas tanks. A Christian group complained that driving SUVs was not in keeping with the teachings of Jesus Christ. Consumer activist Joan Claybrook, head of Public Citizen, charged that SUVs are "a bad bargain for society and a nightmare for American roads." They are, she said, "the dangerous offspring of a heady mix of profit-driven special interest politics and corporate deception."

According to these critics, SUVs are: . . .

- Gas hogs: Their relatively low mileage increases the nation's dependence on foreign oil.
- Pollution machines: They emit more pollutants than smaller cars, thereby increasing global warming and smog.

The only problem with all these pointed barbs is that few of them withstand close scrutiny. . . . Forcing SUVs to be more fuel efficient, or pushing buyers to buy allegedly more sensible smaller cars would have little meaningful impact on the nation's dependence on foreign oil. SUVs aren't increasing air pollution in cities, and their effect on global warming, if any, is negligible. . . .

Because SUVs get less mileage than do cars, critics charge that they contribute to the nation's dependence on foreign oil. Indeed, in the past 10 years, the nation's dependence on imports has climbed from 42% to 54% of oil consumption. Syndicated columnist and book author Arianna Huffington mounted an ad campaign complaining that, because SUVs consume more gasoline than cars, drivers were guilty of supporting the oil-producing regimes in the Persian Gulf—some of which have been accused of providing financial support to terrorists. "What is your SUV doing to our national security?" asked one ad sponsored by Huffington's group, the Detroit Project. At the very least, SUV critics insist that these cars be mandated by the federal government to be more fuel-efficient.

The connection seems to make sense until the data are more closely examined. First, while SUVs generally consume more gasoline than do cars, they are not the rapacious gas hogs critics suggest. True, the largest SUVs get, on average, just 17 miles per gallon. But relatively few of these vehicles sell each year. Indeed, the most popular SUVs are midsize ones, which get an average 20.7 mpg, according to the Oak Ridge National Laboratory. That's just 5 mpg less than a large car, and just 3 mpg less than an average minivan. What's more, despite the surge in sales of SUVs over the past 10 years, overall fuel economy on the road has actually improved.

Consider: In this decade, SUVs went from 5% of all registered cars on the road to 11%. Yet fuel economy of all cars on the road climbed nearly 7% between 1990 and 2000, according to the Oak Ridge National Laboratory. It appears then, that many new car buyers, even those buying SUVs, are trading in less fuel-efficient cars for more fuel-efficient ones. . . .

Fuel Efficiency of 2003 SUVs
(by city and highway MPG)

| Make/Model | MPG | |
Drive train/Engine/Transmission	City	Hwy
Most-Efficient		
Toyota Rav4, 2WD, 4 cyl, Manual	25	31
Toyota Rav4, 2WD, 4 cyl, Automatic	24	29
Least-Efficient		
Cadillac Escalade, AWD, 8 cyl, Automatic	12	16
GMC K1500 Yukon, AWD, 8 cyl, Automatic	12	16
Land Rover Discovery Series II, 4WD, 8 cyl, Automatic	12	16

Environmental Protection Agency, 2003.

Environmentalists argue that dirtier SUVs are creating an intense new air-pollution burden on cities, and contributing to global warming because they emit more carbon dioxide than do more fuel-efficient vehicles. As one environmentalist group puts it: "Sport utility vehicles can spew 30% more carbon monoxide and hydrocarbons and 75% more nitrogen oxides than passenger cars."

These are pollutants that combine with sun and heat to

form smog. The critics note that several popular SUVs get among the lowest rankings for air pollution put out by the Environmental Protection Agency.

Yet, even as SUVs have come to dominate new car sales, air quality has improved. According to the Environmental Protection Agency, the amount of nitrogen oxide in the air dropped 11% between 1992 and 2001. Ozone dropped 3%. Carbon monoxide was down 38%. Those gains came not only as the car market shifted over towards more SUVs, minivans, and light trucks, but as cars overall were driven more. Miles traveled over the past 10 years climbed 30%. The reason may be similar to the reason for the improvements seen over the past decade in overall fuel economy. A driver who trades in a dirty old car for a slightly less polluting new SUV has helped improve the environment, even if the SUV isn't the cleanest new car coming off the assembly line.

The claim that SUVs are contributing meaningfully to global warming is also a stretch. Gasoline consumption in the United States is but one source of so-called greenhouse gases in this country, which themselves are just one source of global greenhouse gas emissions. Assuming that greenhouse gases are warming the planet in a way that will be harmful to humans, a claim that is still subject to much dispute, even eliminating all SUVs would do nothing measurable to warming trends over the next 100 years. All cars on the road account for only about half of oil consumption in this country, and SUVs account for a fraction of that. According to the United Nations, even if all countries in the world cut their emissions of greenhouse gases back to 1990 levels—which would take a far more radical and widespread effort to reduce energy consumption than just making SUVs more efficient—the result would push back eventual temperature increases by roughly 10 years. . . .

In the end, SUVs may not be perfect. And they may not be the sort of car some consumers would choose to buy. But that's the beauty of the free market. Consumers get to decide what cars and what toasters and what homes and what computers best serve their needs. Despite what SUV critics might think, it appears that consumers are making reasonable choices with their hard-earned money.

"Habitat loss, generalization and fragmentation are sprawl's three most damaging impacts on wildlife."

Sprawl Is Harmful to Wildlife

Jutka Terris

The building of houses and businesses in previously unde-veloped areas—suburban sprawl—threatens the existence of numerous species, Jutka Terris opines in the following view-point. According to Terris, the encroachment of humans into fragile ecosystems has sent animals such as the Florida panther and the coastal California gnatcatcher into near-extinction due to the alteration or elimination of their habi-tats. Terris also asserts that the air and water pollution cre-ated by suburban sprawl poses additional threats to wild animals. Terris concludes that conservation measures are needed to protect America's wildlife. Terris is a policy ana-lyst for the National Resources Defense Council, an organi-zation that uses laws and science to protect the environment, and the coauthor of *Solving Sprawl*.

As you read, consider the following questions:

1. According to Terris, what animal and plant species have disappeared from the Sonoran Desert?
2. What is "generalization of habitat"?
3. What are the guiding principles of smart growth, according to the author?

Jutka Terris, "Unwelcome (Human) Neighbors: The Impacts of Sprawl on Wildlife," *Natural Resources Defense Council*, www.nrdc.org, August 1999. Copyright © 2003 by the Natural Resources Council, Inc. Reproduced by permission.

"Bears know their landscape like we know our houses. I have data on one female bear who, I am convinced, has used the same babysitter tree for all the litters of cubs she's had for the last twelve years. Imagine if she woke up after hibernation with her new cubs to find a road and a sprawling suburban neighborhood in place of that tree. What would she do?"

—Susan Morse, forester, carnivore
expert and founder of Keeping Track

Roads and sprawling neighborhoods are replacing pristine wildlife habitats at an alarming pace, putting the survival and reproduction of plants and animals at risk. In just the last few decades, rapidly growing human settlements have consumed large amounts of land in our country, while wildlife habitats have shrunk, fragmented, or disappeared altogether. If the current land use pattern—expansion of built areas at rates much faster than population growth—continues, sprawl could become the problem for U.S. wildlife in the 21st century.

At-Risk Species

First there were tents, then huts, then farmhouses and fields, then towns and cities. Ever since humans set foot on this continent, permanent human settlements have been built and expanded on landscapes that were previously home to wildlife. While loss of habitat to human settlement is not new, the last few decades have seen a dramatic increase in its pace. Nearly one-sixth of the total base of land developed in our country's long history was claimed for development in just 10 years, from 1982 to 1992. But this expansion was not due to an unprecedented population boom in the 80s. Instead, urban sprawl was rapidly outpacing population growth. From 1960 to 1990, the amount of developed land in all U.S. metropolitan areas more than doubled—while population grew by less than 50 percent. Today, this rapid growth continues. Moreover, some of the fastest growth is occurring far beyond our urban areas, in still-rural communities 60 to 70 miles from metropolitan beltways. Such exurbs already account for 60 million people and one-quarter of the recent population growth of the lower 48 states. In the exurbs, developments are often far away from each other, connected only by a system of highways and roads. Such "leapfrog developments" exacerbate the fragmentation of wildlife habitats.

There is wildlife in all these fast-growing areas, metropolitan and rural, and species do not fare well when the natural landscapes are paved over and built on. What kind of wildlife is most at risk? Since sprawl is claiming open lands nationwide across a varied landscape, the species affected by it are also varied.

One victim of sprawl, the Florida panther, is among the most endangered large mammals in the world. It is now reduced to a single population of an estimated 30 to 50 adults. This is especially tragic, considering that the panther—also known as cougar, mountain lion, puma and catamount—was once the most widely distributed mammal (other than humans) in North and South America. In the eastern United States, only the Florida subspecies survives. But for how long? Its southern Florida habitat of hardwood hammocks, pine flatwoods and wetlands is still rapidly giving way to residential developments and agricultural fields. Habitat loss has already driven the Florida panther into a small area, where the few remaining animals are highly inbred, causing such genetic flaws as heart defects and sterility.

In the Southwest, where especially rapid growth is taking place, plant and animal species of the fragile desert ecosystem are at risk. For example, the silent victims of Tucson's rapid expansion into the Sonoran Desert in Arizona include the ancient ironwood, the creosote bush and the graceful saguaro cactus. Growing painfully slowly in the arid lands, these beautiful plants survive for hundreds of years (indeed, some may date back thousands of years). But they take only a few seconds to bulldoze. Disappearing with them are animal species such as the endangered pygmy owl, a beautiful, hand-sized, brown-and-white flecked raptor, and the sonoran pronghorn, a graceful creature that looks like an antelope but is, in fact, the sole survivor of a distinct ancient family dating back 20 million years.

In Southern California, another booming area, the coastal sage ecosystem is unraveling. Sprawling development has wiped out over 90 percent of this landscape, identified by the U.S. Fish and Wildlife Service as "one of the most depleted habitat types in the United States." What is left is badly fragmented and, as a result, the region has experienced a dramatic loss of native species of birds and small mammals. A rare bird with an unfortunately unheroic name, the coastal California gnatcatcher is one that has suffered most. The gnatcatcher has lost some three-fourths of its natural habitat, and its remaining population, now dwindled to perhaps 2,500 pairs, is hanging on in shrinking, isolated patches where it is more exposed to predators. It has recently been classified as a threatened species. The coastal sage ecosystem is also home to such endangered species as the kangaroo rat and the quino checkerspot, a large butterfly with a life cycle that makes it especially vulnerable to habitat loss.

Other species in trouble include the redleg frog and the Pacific pond turtle in Sonoma Valley, California; the piping plover, a tiny bird living and nesting on the Atlantic coast; the dusky salamander in New York state's streams; the hawksbill sea turtle in the Gulf of Mexico; the desert tortoise in the Mojave and Colorado deserts and the nocturnal lynx, with its trademark bobbed tail, in parts of the Northwest and New York state.

Habitats Are Being Destroyed

Before we can talk about change, it is important to understand the many ways that our current patterns of growth hurt wildlife. Habitat loss is one of the most familiar. This concept is perhaps easiest to grasp when a complete transformation of the natural landscape occurs. Almost no on-site wildlife can survive the transition from a meadow to a large new factory, or to an office complex or "big-box" retail outlet surrounded by a vast concrete parking lot. But can wildlife survive when the new use is a residential suburb with some grass and trees? Or an office campus, where buildings are surrounded by green landscaping?

While a few species can adapt to such human-shaped environments, many cannot. And since our suburbs and office campuses are remarkably similar all around the country (and are thus often completely oblivious to their natural surroundings), we are essentially cultivating the few species that do well with irrigated lawns and Norway maples and have learned to eat from our garbage cans and bird feeders. All this is at the expense of the many species that depend on more fragile local habitats.

This trend is called generalization of habitat, and results in the survival of hardy species such as pigeons, squirrels and raccoons. While the overall biomass may not decline—the generalists take over where more sensitive species are disappearing—the total number of species plummets. Standing in a suburban backyard, one may still hear birds singing, but the choir is not nearly as diverse as it was before the subdivisions came and the mature trees were chopped down.

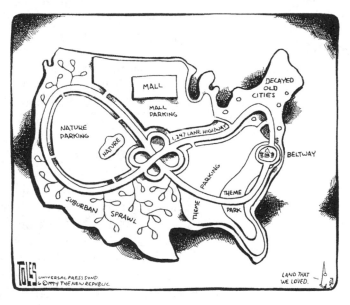

Toles. © 1994 by *The New Republic*. All rights reserved. Reproduced by permission of Universal Press Syndicate.

Another serious problem is habitat fragmentation. When roads, houses and malls break up ecosystems, large populations that once were genetically diverse are broken up into small groups. With amphibians, for example, even a single road across their habitat may be enough to create genetically divergent groups. A result may be a lack of enough genetic variety within each subgroup, resulting in degenerative inbreeding. This has been a significant factor in the decline of the Florida panther, as fragmentation of wetland and forest habitats has resulted in new generations suffering serious, sometimes fatal, genetic flaws.

Fragmentation of habitat may also separate a species from its feeding or breeding grounds. In some cases, not even the first generation survives. Or, a species may survive only until the first environmental stress, such as a drought, occurs, when it is trapped in a small and isolated area. Prior to habitat fragmentation, the thirsty wildlife could find relief at a nearby river during droughts. After development, that river may now be on the other side of a five-lane highway or a strip mall, impossible to reach. The more fragmented, the more vulnerable to any stress an ecosystem is.

Further Effects of Sprawl

Habitat loss, generalization and fragmentation are sprawl's three most damaging impacts on wildlife. But sprawl does more: it also pollutes our rivers, lakes and air, further threatening species. It is easy to see why Michael Klemens of the Wildlife Conservation Society described sprawl as an "extremely severe problem for wildlife," and why ecologist Joseph McAuliffe calls sprawl "an environmental abomination."

Twenty-seven ecosystem types have already declined by as much as 98 percent or more since Europeans settled North America. As of mid-1997, the U.S. Fish and Wildlife Service reported that 1,082 species of plants and animals were listed as threatened and endangered, with another 119 proposed for listing. In a comprehensive assessment of some 20,000 species of plants and animals native to the United States, The Nature Conservancy reports that fully a third are "of conservation concern," believed to be extinct, imperiled or vulnerable. According to the Conservancy, "current extinction rates are conservatively estimated to be at least 10,000 times greater than background levels."

However, not all is lost—yet. The United States still has an abundance of natural areas where wildlife thrives. The question is what we can do now to save them from the rising tide of development.

Conservation Measures

When feasible, buying land that is threatened by development and setting it aside as a nature preserve is a dramatic and secure way to protect some wildlife. But we cannot save our natural areas by land purchases alone: there is simply not enough money to go around. Developers have just as deep, if not deeper, pockets than conservation groups do, and there is too much land around the country that needs to be protected. Buying conservation easements (paying landowners to restrict development on their property) is a more economical approach, but still insufficient.

If money alone won't fix the problem, what about national laws that protect wildlife? The most widely influential of these has been the Endangered Species Act, which has succeeded in rehabilitating some endangered species that are now recovering, among them the bald eagle, the gray wolf, the peregrine falcon, the whooping crane and the mountain lion. Indirectly, the law has also benefited additional species in the protected areas. However, by its nature, the law's scope is limited to the last remaining habitat of the last remaining individuals of a particular species. Surely, we should start protecting our unique ecosystems and dependent species long before the edge of disaster.

Ultimately, purely defensive strategies—setting aside wildlife reserves, attempting to prevent the diminution of endangered species—are insufficient. We need to change the way we plan and manage our growth.

Citizens concerned about sprawl should advocate at least three approaches. First, ecological considerations should play a larger role in our local land use planning decisions. Activities such as mapping wildlife habitats and evaluating a proposed project's impact on those habitats should be routinely incorporated in the planning process. Planners should receive some training in ecology, and interdepartmental cooperation between planners and environmental and wildlife specialists should be encouraged.

Second, ecological thinking does not stop at a local jurisdiction's border; regional cooperation is essential. Ideally, regions should correspond to biological units, such as watersheds, in order to provide maximum benefit for wildlife. This approach has been coined bioregional planning, and has already yielded some promising results. Some states, for example, have designated "areas of critical state concern" based on these areas' unique natural resources. Development in these areas is to be carefully managed, so as to minimize environmental damage, by regional bodies or state agencies. Ecosystems as diverse as New Jersey's pine barrens, Virginia's tidewater region and Florida's wetlands are already enjoying some degree of regional protection.

Third, and perhaps most critically, the ultimate answer to reversing the tide of sprawling development should be to grow differently, to accommodate our housing and commercial needs in a more thoughtful way. The alternative to sprawl, smart growth, is not one simple formula, but rather a set of guiding principles. These should be flexible enough to be adapted to diverse and ever-changing local conditions, and to be achieved by a variety of creative policies and market mechanisms.

Guiding Principles

Among the guiding principles are the following:
- strong central cities and more efficient use of already developed areas;
- compact, walkable developments with several transportation choices;
- a range of housing opportunities and choices; mixed land uses;
- growth management and protection of open spaces.

Maybe the most important lesson for those of us who care deeply about the well-being of our nation's wildlife is that intimate connections exist between the health of our cities (and inner suburbs) and the health of wildlife at the far edges of the metropolitan areas these cities anchor. Protecting open space and wildlife is essential, but not enough, if we want to reverse the damage that urban sprawl inflicts on our wildlife. A more comprehensive approach that aims both to strengthen the urban core and to tame growth at the edge—smart growth—is called for.

*"There may be reasons to decry urban
sprawl or the suburbanization of America,
but the loss of wildlife is not one of them."*

Sprawl Is Not Harmful to Wildlife

Jane S. Shaw

Many environmentalists maintain that the spread of suburbia
into previously rural areas presents a threat to wildlife. In the
following viewpoint Jane S. Shaw argues that these concerns
are unfounded and that deer and other animals are thriving
in newly developed areas. She asserts that suburbanization
benefits wild animals by making it easier for native species to
find food and shelter. While Shaw acknowledges that the in-
flux of animals into suburban areas can cause serious problems, such as attacks by mountain lions, she concludes that
there is no reason to be pessimistic about the ability of wild
animals to survive in suburbia. Shaw is a senior associate of
the Property and Environment Research Center (PERC), an
organization that supports free-market solutions to environmental problems, and the coeditor of *A Guide to Smart
Growth: Shattering Myths and Providing Solutions.*

As you read, consider the following questions:

1. According to Shaw, how do new residents of previously
   rural land establish habitats for wildlife?
2. In James Dunn's opinion, why have counties with large
   cities and suburbs experienced a greater increase in deer
   population than isolated rural counties?
3. In the author's view, how are suburban habitats superior
   to cropland?

A decade ago, who would have thought that New Jersey would host a black bear hunt—the first in 33 years? Or that Virginia, whose population of bald eagles was once down to 32 breeding pairs, would have 329 known active bald eagle nests? Who would have expected *Metropolitan Home* magazine to be advising its readers about ornamental grasses to keep away white-tailed deer, now found in the millions around the country?

Such incidents illustrate a transformed America. This nation, often condemned for being crowded, paved over, and studded with nature-strangling shopping malls, is proving to be a haven for wild animals.

An Upsurge of Wild Animals

It is difficult to ignore this upsurge of wildlife, because stories about bears raiding trashcans and mountain lions sighted in subdivisions frequently turn up in the press or on television. Featured in these stories are animals as large as moose, as well as once-threatened birds such as eagles and falcons and smaller animals like wolverines and coyotes.

One interpretation of these events is that people are moving closer to wilderness and invading the territory of wild animals. But this is only a small part of the story. As this essay will show, wild animals increasingly find suburban life in the United States to be attractive.

The stories, while fascinating, are not all upbeat. Americans are grappling with new problems—the growing hazard of automobile collisions with deer, debates over the role of hunting, the disappearance of fragile wild plants gobbled up by hungry ruminants, and even occasional human deaths caused by these animals.

At the same time, the proliferation of wildlife should assure Americans that the claim that urban sprawl is wiping out wildlife is simply poppycock. Human settlement in the early 21st century may be sprawling and suburban—about half the people in this country live in suburbs—but it is more compatible with wildlife than most people think. There may be reasons to decry urban sprawl or the suburbanization of America, but the loss of wildlife is not one of them.

Two phenomena are fueling this increase in wild animals.

One is natural reforestation, especially in the eastern United States. This is largely a result of the steady decline in farming, including cotton farming, a decline that allows forests to retake territory they lost centuries ago. The other is suburbanization, the expansion of low-density development outside cities, which provides a variety of landscapes and vegetation that attract animals. Both trends undermine the claim that wild open spaces are being strangled and that habitat for wild animals is shrinking.

The trend toward regrowth of forest has been well-documented. The percent of forested land in New Hampshire increased from 50 percent in the 1880s to 86 percent 100 years later.

Forested land in Connecticut, Massachusetts, and Rhode Island increased from 35 percent to 59 percent over that same period. "The same story has been repeated in other places in the East, the South, and the Lake States," writes forestry expert Roger Sedjo.

Environmentalist Bill McKibben exulted in this "unintentional and mostly unnoticed renewal of the rural and mountainous East" in a 1995 article in the *Atlantic Monthly*. Calling the change "the great environmental story of the United States, and in some ways of the whole world," he added, "Here, where 'suburb' and 'megalopolis' were added to the world's vocabulary, an explosion of green is under way." Along with the reforestation come the animals; McKibben cites a moose "ten miles from Boston," as well as an eastern United States full of black bears, deer, alligators, and perhaps even mountain lions.

This re-greening of the eastern United States explains why some large wild animals are thriving, but much of the wildlife Americans are seeing today is a direct result of the suburbs. Clearly, suburban habitat is not sterile.

The Return of Deer

When people move onto what once was rural land, they modify the landscape. Yes, they build more streets, more parking lots, and more buildings. Wetlands may be drained, hayfields may disappear, trees may be cut down, and pets may proliferate. At the same time, however, the new residents will create habitat for wildlife. They will create ponds, establish gardens, plant trees, and set up bird nesting-boxes. Ornamental nurseries and truck farms may replace cropland, and parks may replace hedgerows.

This new ecology is different, but it is often friendly to animals, especially those that University of Florida biologist Larry Harris calls "meso-mammals," or mammals of medium size. They do not need broad territory for roaming to find food, as moose and grizzly bears do. They can find places in the suburbs to feed, nest, and thrive, especially where gardens flourish.

One example of the positive impact of growth is the rebound of the endangered Key deer, a small white-tailed deer found only in Florida and named for the Florida Keys. According to *Audubon* magazine, the Key deer is experiencing a "remarkable recovery." The news report continues: "Paradoxically, part of the reason for the deer's comeback may lie in the increasing development of the area." Paraphrasing the remarks of a university researcher, the reporter says that human development "tends to open up overgrown forested areas and provide vegetation at deer level—the same factors fueling deer population booms in suburbs all over the country."

Indeed, white-tailed deer of normal size are the most prominent species proliferating in the suburbs. In the *New York Times*, reporter Andrew C. Revkin has commented that "suburbanization created a browser's paradise: a vast patchwork of well-watered, fertilizer-fattened plantings to feed on and vest-pocket forests to hide in, with hunters banished to more distant woods."

The increase in the number of deer in the United States is so great that many people, especially wildlife professionals, are trying to figure out what to do about them. In 1997, the Wildlife Society, a professional association of wildlife biologists, devoted a special 600-page issue of its *Bulletin* to "deer overabundance." The lead article noted, "We hear more each year about the high costs of crop and tree-seedling damage, deer-vehicle collisions, and nuisance deer in suburban locales." Insurance companies are worried about the increase in damage from automobile collisions with deer and similar-sized animals. And there are fears that the increase in deer in populated areas means that the deer tick could be causing the increased number of reported cases of Lyme disease.

Yes, the proliferation of deer poses problems, as do geese, whose flocks can foul ponds and lawns and are notorious nuisances on golf courses, and beaver, which can cut down groves of trees. Yet the proliferation of deer is also a wildlife success story. At least that is the view of Robert J. Warren, editor of the *Bulletin*, who calls the resurgence of deer "one of the premier examples of successful wildlife management." Today's deer population in the United States may be as high as 25 million, says Richard Nelson, writing in *Sports Afield*.

No Threat to Farmland

One frequently cited rationale for smart growth regulation is that suburban development allegedly is eating up America's farmland, threatening the agriculture industry and even our ability to feed ourselves in the future. This purported market failure must be remedied by regulatory restrictions on suburban development.

The facts are that non-agriculture uses of land in the U.S.—cities, highways, railroads, airports—amount to just 3.6% (82,000,000 acres) of the total land, and cropland has remained virtually constant, at 24% of the U.S. land mass, since 1945. Over three-fourths of the states have more than 90% of their land in rural uses—including forests, cropland, pastures, wildlife reserves, and parks—and just 4.8% of the total land area of the U.S. is developed.

Thomas J. Dilorenzo, *USA Today Magazine*, May 2000.

People have mixed feelings about deer. In the *Wildlife Society Bulletin*, Dale R. McCullough and his colleagues reported on a survey of households in El Cerrito and Kensington, two communities near Berkeley, California. Twenty-eight percent of those who responded reported severe damage to vegetation by the deer, and 25 percent reported moderate damage. Forty-two percent liked having the deer around, while 35 percent disliked them and 24 percent were indifferent. The authors summarized the findings by saying: "As expected, some residents loved deer, whereas others considered them 'hoofed rats.'"

James Dunn, a geologist who has studied wildlife in New York State, believes that suburban habitat fosters deer more than forests do. Dunn cites statistics on the harvest of buck deer reported by the New York State government. Since 1970 the deer population has multiplied 7.1 times in suburban areas (an increase of 610 percent), but only 3.4 times (an increase of 240 percent) in the state overall.

Other Suburban Species

Dunn explains that the forests have been allowed to regrow without logging or burning, so they lack the "edge" that allows sunlight in and encourages vegetation suitable for deer. In his view, that explains why counties with big cities (and therefore with suburbs) have seen a greater increase in deer populations than have the isolated, forested rural counties. Supporting this point, Andrew Revkin quotes a wildlife biologist at the National Zoo in Washington, D.C., "Deer are an edge species," he says, "and the world is one big edge now."

Deer are not the only wild animals that turn up on lawns and doorsteps, however. James Dunn lists species in the Albany, New York, suburbs in addition to deer: birds such as robins, woodpeckers, chickadees, grouse, finches, hawks, crows, and nuthatches, as well as squirrels, chipmunks, opossums, raccoons, foxes, and rabbits. Deer attract coyotes too. According to a 1999 article in *Audubon*, biologists estimate that the coyote population (observed in all states except Hawaii) is about double what it was in 1850.

Joel Garreau, author of *Edge City*, includes black bears, red-tailed hawks, peregrine falcons, and beaver on his list of animals that find suburban niches. Garreau still considers these distant "edge city" towns a "far less diverse ecology than what was there before." However, he writes, "if you measure it by the standard of city, it is a far more diverse ecology than anything humans have built in centuries, if not millennia."

For one reason or another, some environmental activists tend to dismiss the resurgence of deer and other wildlife. In an article criticizing suburban sprawl, Carl Pope, executive director of the Sierra Club, says that the suburbs are "very good for the most adaptable and common creatures—raccoons, deer, sparrows, starlings, and sea gulls" but "devastating for wildlife that is more dependent upon privacy, seclusion, and protection from such predators as dogs and cats."

Yet the suburbs attract animals larger than meso-mammals, and the suburban habitat may be richer than what they replace. In many regions, suburban growth comes at the expense of agricultural land that was cultivated for decades, even centuries. Cropland doesn't necessarily provide abundant habitat. Environmental essayist Donald Worster, for example, has little favorable to say about land cultivated for crops or used for livestock grazing. In Worster's view, there was a time when agriculture was diversified, with small patches of different crops and a variety of animals affecting the landscape. Not now. "The trend over the past two hundred years or so," he writes, "has been toward the establishment of monocultures on every continent." In contrast, suburbs are not monocultures.

Even large animals can be found at the edges of metropolitan areas. Early in 2004, a mountain lion attacked a woman riding a bicycle in the Whiting Ranch Wilderness Park in the foothills above populous Orange County, and the same animal may have killed a man who was found dead nearby. According to the *Los Angeles Times*, if the man's death is confirmed as caused by the mountain lion, it would be the first death by a mountain lion in Orange County. The *Times* added, however, that "mountain lions are no strangers in Orange County's canyons and wilderness parks." Indeed, in 1994, mountain lions killed two women in state parks near San Diego and Sacramento. Deer may be attracting the cats, suggests Paul Beier, a professor at the University of California at Berkeley. . . .

Learning to Live with Animals

The fact that wildlife finds a home in suburban settings does not mean that all wildlife will do so. The greening of the suburbs is no substitute for big stretches of land—both public and private—that allow large mammals such as grizzly bears, elk, antelope, and caribou to roam. The point of this essay is that the suburbs offer an environment that is appealing to many wild animal species.

If the United States continues to prosper, the 21st century

is likely to be an environmental century. Affluent people will seek to maintain or, in some cases, restore an environment that is attractive to wildlife, and more parks will likely be nestled within suburban developments, along with gardens, arboreta, and environmentally compatible golf courses. As wildlife proliferates, Americans will learn to live harmoniously with more birds and meso-mammals. New organizations and entrepreneurs will help integrate nature into the human landscape. There is no reason to be pessimistic about the ability of wildlife to survive and thrive in the suburbs.

Periodical Bibliography

The following articles have been selected to supplement the diverse views presented in this chapter.

Chris Baker and Gary Anderson — "Power Hungry People," *Insight on the News*, June 25, 2001.

Linda Baker — "The Fast-Moving Fight to Stop Urban Sprawl," *E: The Environmental Magazine*, May 2000.

Rich Ceppos — "Buy What You Want," *Auto Week*, September 15, 2003.

Marla Cone — "Vehicles Blamed for a Greater Share of Smog," *Los Angeles Times*, October 30, 1999.

Thomas J. Dilorenzo — "The Myth of Suburban Sprawl," *USA Today Magazine*, May 2000.

Peter W. Huber and Mark P. Mills — "How Cities Green the Planet," *City Journal*, Winter 2000.

Robert W. Kates — "Population and Consumption," *Environment*, April 2000.

Jane Holtz Kay — "Cars Are Key to Global Warming," *Progressive Populist*, June 15, 2000.

Charles Komanoff et al. — "Car Talk," *Amicus Journal*, Fall 1999.

Jim Motavalli and Josh Harkinson — "Buying Green," *E: The Environmental Magazine*, September/October 2002.

Randal O'Toole — "Too Smart for Our Own Good," *Liberty*, May 1999.

Alejandro Reuss — "Car Trouble," *Dollars & Sense*, March/April 2003.

Wall Street Journal — "Gas Attack," March 28, 2000.

Dan Whipple — "Greenprinting for Success," *Land & People*, Fall 2001.

CHAPTER 4

What Policies Will Improve the Environment?

Chapter Preface

The search for effective environmental policies often leads to a debate as to whether a free market and a healthy environment are compatible. One example of this discussion concerns the impact free trade has on the environment. While some promarket environmentalists assert that free trade should be encouraged, other people argue that it will worsen the health of the planet by increasing pollution in poorer countries.

Free trade advocates argue that involving poorer nations in the global economy will help reduce pollution in those countries. According to Daniel K. Benjamin, an economics professor at Clemson University, studies indicate "that for each one percent that freer trade raises per capita income in a nation, the result is that pollution (as measured by sulfur dioxide concentrations) falls by one percent." Daniel T. Griswold, the associate director of the Cato Institute's Center for Trade Policy Studies, also contends that the wealth created by free trade helps reduce pollution because it allows developing countries to afford higher environmental standards. According to Griswold, "When a sizeable share of the population lives on the edge of subsistence, pristine air and water are luxuries, not necessities. Economic development must come first."

On the other hand, critics of free trade maintain that the United States and other industrialized nations will exploit looser trade laws and create "pollution havens" in poorer nations. According to these environmentalists, wealthy nations will relocate polluting industries to impoverished countries that have lax environmental standards. In consequence, they argue, free trade cannot be achieved without significant damage to the environment. In an article on the Web site GreenBiz.com, Kumar Venkat encapsulates this view when he writes,

> Pollution from transportation and consumption of goods, as well as resource use throughout the life cycles of products, are all potentially major avenues through which global trade can damage the environment. When all these effects are combined with production-driven pollution, the final out-

come could easily reverse the optimistic result that trade benefits the environment.

The full impact that free trade will have on the environment is not yet evident. In the following chapter the authors debate several environmental policies; these debates often involve free market advocates arguing against more traditional environmentalists. The essential points of contention are often the same no matter which policy is being debated or whether the policy has a national or global reach.

"Pollution-credit trading is an inherently capitalist approach to the global warming problem."

Emissions Trading Will Improve the Environment

Ricardo Bayon

Many people believe that global warming is the most serious environmental problem facing the world today. In the following viewpoint Ricardo Bayon argues that the best way to ameliorate global warming is by establishing a market to trade carbon dioxide emissions. In this market, energy companies whose plants exceed emissions standards set by the Environmental Protection Agency could buy emissions credits from companies whose plants are emitting less than the standards. According to Bayon, allowing companies to reduce pollution by buying and selling emissions credits is a proven solution. Indeed, sulfur dioxide trading has reduced acid rain. He contends that by placing a cap on carbon dioxide emissions, the government will enable the carbon dioxide trading market, which has already begun in the private sector, to thrive. Bayon is a fellow at the New America Foundation, a nonpartisan think tank based in Washington.

As you read, consider the following questions:

1. Why was the sulfur dioxide trading program created, according to the author?
2. In the author's view what lesson might be learned in the first decade of the twenty-first century?

Gary Payne and Jeremy Taylor are two Wall Street types who work for trading companies in, respectively, Kansas City and Houston. Their daily routine is familiar to speculative traders everywhere: They wake up early to get a jump on the markets, read the industry papers, take a look at their companies' trading portfolios, and log onto their Bloomberg terminals to see who's buying and who's selling. But they do not trade in stocks, bonds, currencies or even pork bellies.

Instead, what Payne and Taylor trade is the right to pollute—specifically, the government-given right to emit sulfur dioxide (SO_2) and nitrogen oxides, the two gases chiefly responsible for acid rain.

Successfully Selling Sulfur Dioxide

In a classic example of doing well by doing good, successful traders such as Payne and Taylor buy pollution credits low, sell them high and make money—all the while playing an integral role in a system that has reduced annual emissions of SO_2 by U.S. utilities by 29 percent since 1990. Their experience offers a valuable lesson for U.S. policy makers seeking solutions to the problem of global climate change. The sulfur dioxide market provides a business-friendly, market-oriented, cost-effective model for reducing emissions of carbon dioxide, the gas generally considered to be the main culprit behind global warming.

The market is based on the same theory as the country-to-country emissions trading program envisioned in the Kyoto Protocol signed by 178 countries and rejected by President [George W.] Bush. But the president should not be put off by this. Pollution-credit trading is an inherently capitalist approach to the global warming problem that can be set up nationally (or regionally, with Canada and Mexico) and can be tailored to U.S. needs.

Perhaps the administration needs to be reminded of the successes of the SO_2 program. It was created to combat acid rain, one of the major environmental issues of the 1980s. Acid rain is caused when sulfur dioxide and nitrogen oxides are emitted into the atmosphere, mostly by power generators. In 1990, Congress amended the Clean Air Act to set national targets for emissions of those gases; it then instructed the Environmental Protection Agency (EPA) to allocate the rights to these limited emissions among major U.S. utilities, and to create a mechanism for the utilities to buy and sell those rights. Note that the government did not tell utilities how to reduce their emissions of SO_2. It merely set targets and let the market determine how best to achieve this goal. So, under the EPA plan, a power plant that was emitting too much sulfur dioxide had several options: It could install less polluting technology, it could switch its fuel from coal to natural gas (which produces less SO_2), or it could purchase excess emission credits from another utility. A utility that upgraded its technology or switched fuels might even cover some of the costs by selling emission credits it no longer needed.

Trading in sulfur dioxide rights got fully underway in 1995 (and in nitrogen oxides some years later). Today, the right to emit SO_2 sells for around $200 a ton and is sold in lots of 2,500 tons, which means it is available to anyone with half a million dollars to spare. The big buyers and sellers are utilities and energy companies, but there are exceptions. The venerable Wall Street brokerage firm Cantor Fitzgerald once helped a wealthy benefactor purchase the right to emit one ton of SO_2 as a wedding present for a pair of environmentalists; and it brokered a deal for an environmental group that wanted to give its retirees emission rights instead of gold watches.

Taylor, who tracks the market closely, says that in the past year about $668 million worth of SO_2 credits changed hands. He points out, however, that if the trading in SO_2 options and futures is included, the total market is several times that size. "You can buy SO_2 puts, calls, straddles, call spreads, whatever you need," he says.

Positive Effects on the Environment

And this robust and liquid market is not just profitable; it also has been remarkably effective at controlling acid rain. According to the EPA, which tracks the emissions of 263 of the largest power plants in the country, they emitted 8.7 million tons of SO_2 in 1990, when Congress first mandated a cap. That figure dropped to 7.4 million tons by 1994. But in 1995, when trading in SO_2 credits began, emissions plummeted to 4.5 million tons, even though power generation continued to increase. In the Northeast and Mid-Atlantic regions of the United States, where acid rain and lake acidification were particularly problematic, acid rain levels declined by 25 percent between 1995 and 1999.

The cost to businesses of this environmental benefit was barely more than a tenth of what had originally been predicted. Before Congress mandated the sulfur dioxide cap, the Edison Electric Institute estimated that it would cost $7.4 billion a year for industry to meet its targets; over the ensuing decade, successive studies by a variety of groups have shown that the real figure is likely to be closer to $870 million a year.

In other words, the SO_2 market is doing what markets do best: It has wrung inefficiencies out of the system and allocated scarce resources (in this case, pollution rights) very cost-effectively.

Encouraging Carbon Dioxide Trading

Markets can do the same thing for carbon dioxide. But this will require of President Bush and Congress at least one act of political courage: They will need to cap CO_2 emissions. Bush pledged to do so during his 2000 campaign, but later reversed his stance. Now he would have to reverse the reversal—but he can find inspiration in his father, the first President Bush, whose administration launched the successful SO_2 trading program. [As of February 2004, a cap had not been set.]

Besides, the gesture might not be as difficult as it looks—because when it comes to greenhouse gases, business is way ahead of government. A quiet "gray market" already exists in carbon dioxide. Individual companies, expecting some kind of government regulation in the not-too-distant future, have been buying and selling CO_2 credits for more than three years. "If you are a large power company spending millions of dollars building plants that you expect to operate for 20 or 30 years," says CO_2 trader Carlton Bartels, "you are not happy when government comes along and tells you not to worry about global warming, at least not for the next four years. That doesn't decrease the risks your company faces as a result of climate change. It may actually increase them."

Bartels is chief executive officer of CO2e.com, a carbon dioxide trading firm that was spun off from Cantor Fitzgerald [in early 2001]. The new company helps businesses prepare for what Bartels calls the inevitable "carbon-constrained" future—when public pressure will force governments to regulate emissions of the gases that cause climate change.

Pollution Permits Throughout the World

Consider Costa Rica, which once allowed one of the world's highest rates of deforestation. In a revolutionary turnaround, that government has been paying private landowners for the water-filtration, climate-stabilization, and other services provided by forests they maintain. More than $100,000,000 has been disbursed.

Costa Rica also helped launch the odd global commodity known as a carbon credit. A kind of pollution permit, it is a measure of a reduction in emissions of carbon dioxide, a leading greenhouse gas. Such a reduction can be achieved by investing in energy-saving technology or, under some conditions, planting new forests. The Kyoto Protocol—the international treaty to combat global warming—recognizes carbon credits, and exchanges to trade them are being set up worldwide, including in Great Britain and Chicago.

Katherine Ellison and Gretchen Daily, *USA Today Magazine*, March 2003.

In the meantime, CO2e.com is busy arranging trades for companies that want to stay ahead of the curve. For example, Houston-based Petro Source Carbon Co. has constructed a pipeline that takes the carbon dioxide produced by four U.S. power plants and pumps it into new oil wells in west Texas, where it enhances oil recovery. Since the CO_2 it uses would otherwise be vented into the atmosphere, Petro Source figures it will have carbon credits to spare if and when the United States puts a cap on CO_2 emissions. Meanwhile, Ontario Power Generation of Toronto, whose plants emit carbon dioxide, expects Canada to institute a similar cap. In a deal brokered by CO2e.com, Ontario Power recently bought 1.3 million tons of Petro Source's credits. Both parties expect their governments to honor the deal in the future.

Bartels estimates that in its short lifetime, CO2e.com has been involved in trades for the equivalent of 3.5 million tons of CO_2 emissions rights, each ton selling for between $1 and $5 a ton. (A ton of carbon dioxide is much cheaper than a ton of sulfur dioxide, in part, because trade in CO_2 is still highly speculative. If governments institute CO_2 emissions caps, these prices should skyrocket.) Even before CO2e.com was created, he said, Cantor Fitzgerald helped move between 20 million and 30 million tons of CO_2 emissions rights.

By the end of this decade, Bartels believes that the CO_2 market could be worth tens of billions of dollars. "Given the amount of global emissions," he says, "this could become the largest commodity market in the world."

As President Bush seeks a coherent policy on climate change, he would do well to realize that Wall Street, power companies and emissions traders have for years been sitting on an elegant—not to mention profitable—solution to his problems. The 1980s may have taught us that greed is not always good, but the decade to come is likely to show that it can sometimes be green.

"The result of the online market for greenhouse gas emissions may well be that profit trumps public health and environmental concerns once again."

Emissions Trading May Worsen the Environment

Claire Barliant and Mike Burger

Emissions trading involves low-polluting companies selling unused pollution credits, which specify how much pollution smokestacks can emit, to heavy-polluting companies. Allowing companies to buy and sell the right to emit carbon dioxide will likely worsen the environment, Claire Barliant and Mike Burger claim in the following viewpoint. They assert that the effectiveness of pollution credit trades is nearly impossible to verify because these trades occur without any third-party monitoring. In addition, Barliant and Burger contend that emissions trading offers no incentive for heavy polluters to clean up their act. Barliant and Burger are writers for *Village Voice*.

As you read, consider the following questions:
1. What is the price range of pollution credits, according to Barliant and Burger?
2. In the authors' opinion why do direct exchanges raise questions of reliability?
3. What groups will be most affected by increased levels of pollution, according to the authors?

As protesters outside global-warming talks in The Hague [in November 2000] built sandbag dikes to protest the predicted rise in sea levels, a crowd of brokers, consultants, and engineers gathered across town for an old-fashioned launch party. CO2e.com was gearing up to capitalize on the emerging trillion-dollar market in greenhouse gases.

Companies Are Taking Action

The online exchange, created by brokerage firm Cantor Fitzgerald and PriceWaterhouseCoopers, has a new take on the old model of trading the rights to pollute. For the past decade, companies have bought and sold pollution credits, which specify how many tons of acid-rain chemicals a smokestack can emit. Under that system, a relatively clean manufacturer can sell unused credits to a refinery that can't meet its limits. Most of those transactions have occurred within the United States, and most have relied on brokers who ensure that buyer and seller operate in good faith. Now, the 170 countries behind the 1997 Kyoto Protocol [which sought to reduce global warming] are seeking to trade greenhouse gases as well, though negotiators have never been able to hammer out an agreement for how these international exchanges would work.

Yet companies, through brokers and business-to-business exchanges like CO2e, are jumping in early, trying to beat governments to the regulatory punch. An estimated 160 million tons of carbon dioxide have already changed hands through 60-plus trades offline. Companies expect to get credit for the moved tons under whatever international rules are eventually set down. In Canada, some government officials have talked to industrial players about getting credit for early action. "If you're a buyer," says one industry insider, "then you're doing it to offset future regulatory requirements."

Corporations have another motivation for taking the initiative: buy low, pollute high. Right now, companies can buy the credit to emit carbon dioxide for anywhere between $1 and $4 a ton. Natsource, a broker in carbon dioxide and other emissions, estimates that reductions now worth $600,000 could reach prices as high as $12 million in an official market.

No Standards or Reliability

At the moment, however, there are no standards that define what a reduction actually is. Nor are there sanctioned—or, in most cases, even unsanctioned—third parties overseeing trades. Without a third party monitoring the transactions, verifying and tracking promised reductions can be difficult.

Typically, a broker handles the tricky issues that arise between buyers and sellers of carbon dioxide. Moreover, the broker can insure that the deal is legit. But outfits like CO2e are creating tech-based marketplaces where brokers recede into the background. "There's no human involved," says Walter Alcorn of GreenOnline, a company that sells software to facilitate Web-based exchanges. "Trades are done automatically by computer."

Direct exchanges, though efficient, raise questions of reliability, even when no money changes hands. During the [2000] presidential election, sites like Votetrader.org and Voteswap.org encouraged Green Party supporters in swing states to vote for Al Gore in exchange for Ralph Nader votes in states safely in the Democrat's pocket. The ultimate goal was to raise the Green Party's share of the popular vote to 5 percent, so it would qualify for federal matching funds in 2004. But state attorneys general—and Nader himself—rejected the concept of swapping ballots over the Internet, because the trades were impossible to verify. Someone looking to take out Nader votes could have pledged a single vote multiple times.

For now, proponents of greenhouse gas emissions trading do not seem particularly concerned about shams. "There's a great irony," says CO2e chief Carlton Bartels. "Everybody is suspicious of the program. [But] my clients are spending millions of dollars. They're not going to walk away with a promise. They want title. And if you don't deliver, they want penalties."

To others, a system that lacks a third party vetting the deal seems rife with potential problems. Luke Cole, general counsel at the San Francisco–based Center on Race, Poverty, and the Environment, says emission-trading programs "are shot through with fraud and very difficult to monitor and enforce."

Pollution Credits Fail

Once the EPA [Environmental Protection Agency] actually began auctioning pollution credits in 1993 it became clear that virtually nothing was going according to their projections. The first pollution credits sold for between $122 and $310, significantly less than the agency's estimated minimum price, and by 1995, bids at the EPA's annual auction of sulfur dioxide allowances averaged around $130 per ton of emissions. As the value of the credits declines, the incentive to buy credits rather than invest in pollution controls becomes increasingly attractive. Air quality can continue to decline, as companies in some parts of the country simply buy their way out of having to comply with pollution reductions.

Brian Tokar, *Dollars & Sense*, March/April 1996.

Companies involved in the premarket market hope the system and expertise they develop will be adopted by countries once the conditions of the Kyoto Protocol are finalized.[1] "If we're strict enough, and the government and environmental community comes and looks at our protocols, they'll actually adopt them," says Bartels. "You can't write those things without experiments." But some activists believe these experimenters are trying to set standards they like before governments can step in. "This means that the foxes are designing the henhouse," says Cole. "They're going to know exactly where the loopholes are and where the back exits are."

Trading Away Health

Environmentalists and European negotiators in The Hague wrangled over capping emissions within individual countries. Already the world's leader in greenhouse gas emissions, the United States wants to allow unlimited trading on an international exchange, so its industries can buy as many credits and spew as much pollution as they want. But under those rules, a country like Russia, where emissions are well below the requirements, would have little incentive to cut pollution, while America could continue fouling the air with yet more tons of carbon dioxide. Everyone in the States will be affected by this, but the real burden falls on the poor and disenfranchised. "We

1. As of July 2004, the protocol had not been finalized.

know [factories] are primarily in communities of color," says Cole. "So now these communities would be responsible for not just their country's, but the world's pollution."

The result of the online market for greenhouse gas emissions may well be that profit trumps public health and environmental concerns once again. Trading the right to pollute online is not the same as trading limited-edition Barbies on eBay. Nor is it the same as other business-to-business exchanges for industrial or corporate goods. The commodity here is public property—public health, the ozone layer, climatic stability. If the Kyoto Protocol is ratified by Congress—and that's a stretch of the imagination—greenhouse gases may well grow to be the next megabucks market.[2] But at what cost to the environment?

"In any market economy, you have winners and losers," says Cole. "What you're creating here is a whole other market scheme. And we know who the losers are going to be."

2. The United States has not ratified the protocol.

"The Endangered Species Act is a dynamic and flexible law that continues to work."

The Endangered Species Act Should Be Preserved

John D. Dingell

John D. Dingell, a Democrat from Michigan, is the most senior member of the House of Representatives and the author of the Endangered Species Act (ESA). In the following viewpoint Dingell asserts that the ESA remains a sensible and powerful law that has increased or stabilized the population of numerous species and should not be weakened. He maintains that President George W. Bush and Republican politicians are misguided in their efforts to roll back the ESA and create exemptions for the military. Dingell concludes that Congress needs to preserve the act for at least thirty more years.

As you read, consider the following questions:
1. According to Dingell, what message did the United States send through the enactment of the Endangered Species Act?
2. Why is the author outraged by claims by the Bush administration that conservation laws make it more difficult to fight the war on terror?
3. Why is the preservation of America's natural heritage personally important to Dingell?

On December 28, 1973, I watched President Richard Nixon sign into law the Endangered Species Act. It was one of my proudest moments in Congress. For 30 years the ESA has been protecting our environment and species on the verge of extinction.

Today, conservationists and supporters look at the ESA and call its enactment visionary, while developers and critics refer to it in four-letter terms not fit for printing on the pages of this newspaper [*Rocky Mountain News*]. I disagree with both characterizations.

Sensible and Flexible

To me, the ESA was and remains common sense. Like many of the cornerstone environmental laws we put in place during the early 1970s, the ESA's enactment was a nonpartisan, consensus undertaking: it passed the House by a vote of 391–12, and the Senate by a vote of 92–0.

The ESA and its overwhelming passage by Congress remain a prime example of our nation's long, proud tradition of respect for our wildlife and natural resources. In enacting ESA, the United States sent a strong message to the world by putting our nation on the forefront of protecting wildlife in an effort to make our own habitat a bit better. Ours was the first nation to say that only natural extinction is part of the natural order and that extinction caused by human neglect and interference should be prevented to the maximum extent possible.

Most importantly, the Endangered Species Act is a dynamic and flexible law that continues to work. [As of December 2003,] 14 species have been recovered, including the peregrine falcon and the gray whale. This occurred notwithstanding the fact that a species is not typically listed until its population is extremely depleted. Another measure of success is the fact that 41 percent of the listed species have improved or stabilized their population.

Military Exemptions Are Wrong

Despite the success of the ESA and its bipartisan origins, the law begins its fourth decade under a quiet, yet dangerous assault. The Bush administration and the Republican leadership in Congress have undertaken a sustained effort to roll back the ESA and create vast carve-outs for the Defense Department and numerous special interests.

In the last decade we have seen the American military at its most effective. Our armed forces have won two major wars in Iraq, toppled the Taliban in Afghanistan, stopped a civil war in Yugoslavia, and prevented genocide in Kosovo. All these missions were trained for with the ESA intact. Yet, now the administration appears to be saying that desert tortoise preservation is a threat to our national security, and that this nation's conservation laws weaken our ability to wage the war on terror.

Number of U.S. Listed Endangered and Threatened Species, by Major Group, 1995–1999

	1995	1996	1997	1998	1999
Mammals	66	66	66	69	69
Birds	91	90	93	93	89
Reptiles	33	33	36	36	38
Amphibians	12	13	16	16	17
Fish	105	107	108	119	112
Crustaceans	17	17	19	20	20
Snails	22	22	22	28	28
Insects	29	29	37	37	37
Arachnids	5	5	5	5	5
Clams	57	57	62	69	69
Plants	525	614	668	702	721
Total	962	1,053	1,132	1,194	1,205

U.S. Department of the Interior, Fish and Wildlife Service, 2000.

This is an outrageous claim that not only gives short shrift to the abilities of our military personnel, but also completely ignores the fact that the ESA already contains exemptions for national security. Under the act, should the Secretary of Defense request a waiver for national security, a committee—comprising a number of cabinet secretaries, agency directors and representatives of the states—is required to not only review the request but also grant it.

Unfortunately, the Bush administration never attempted to take advantage of the waiver process we very purposefully built into the ESA. Instead, the administration quietly stuck a rider onto [2003's] defense authorization bill that essentially carved the Defense Department and its millions of acres of land out of the act. The rider allows the military a much lower standard than the current law and, ultimately, will likely shift the burden of providing for the recovery of endangered species to private landowners.

But efforts to narrow the law and undo the ESA have not been confined solely to domestic exemptions for the military. The administration recently announced an effort to roll back the act's prohibition on importing endangered species from abroad. This is simply wrong.

The act's prohibition on importing endangered species helped prevent the extinction of the African elephant that was being decimated out of greed for its ivory tusks, and it has served to protect other magnificent animals including the rhinoceros, the Bengal tiger, and the humpback whale.

Keep the Law Intact

Because of these assaults on the Endangered Species Act, [in November 2003] I joined with other legislators in signing a pledge to uphold the act for another 30 years to ensure that it will continue to protect our land, wildlife and natural resources for our children and grandchildren to enjoy. I hope that other members of Congress, regardless of party affiliation, will also lend themselves to this fight to keep the ESA from becoming endangered.

The Endangered Species Act has been successful now for 30 years. Without it, there might not be a single bald eagle or peregrine falcon in our skies; no manatees or cutthroat trout in our waters; no gray wolves or grizzly bears in our forests. And, the ESA preserved our natural heritage during a time in which the U.S. economy grew at record rates. This is critically important to me as an avid hunter and sportsman who represents a congressional district primarily dependent upon development and manufacturing growth for its well-being.

As we close out the first 30 years of the Endangered Species Act and open the door to the next, our goal should be to maintain the integrity of the law. The ESA has all the tools in it we need to protect our natural environment, while promoting our national economy—and that's something well worth preserving.

"The [Endangered Species Act] has failed in its mission to recover threatened and endangered species."

The Endangered Species Act Must Be Reformed

Ike C. Sugg

The Endangered Species Act (ESA) is a complete failure that has caused considerable inconvenience to many landowners, Ike C. Sugg asserts in the following viewpoint. According to Sugg, species that are purportedly protected by the act are far more likely to become extinct under it than to recover. Because the ESA penalizes private landowners who have endangered species residing on their property by restricting land use, it encourages landowners to view endangered species as enemies, Sugg contends. Sugg is a fellow at the Competitive Enterprise Institute, an organization that supports the use of private property rights to protect the environment, and the former executive director of the Exotic Wildlife Association.

As you read, consider the following questions:
1. How has the Endangered Species Act produced opponents of wildlife, according to Sugg?
2. According to the author, how many species have been removed from the ESA's list of protected species?
3. In Sugg's opinion what is the main goal of ESA reform?

Kings, queens, feudal lords, and dictators used to decide who, if anyone, could use which resources, for what purpose, at what price, and to what extent. That antiquated system of centralized command and control over wildlife remains throughout much of the world today, but it is weakening. The "king's game" approach to wildlife conservation, wherein government ownership and prohibitions rule, is going the way of the dodo, much like monarchy itself. But here in the United States, that transition away from the king's game is occurring at glacial speed, primarily because the U.S. environmental establishment is committed to ensuring that indigenous wildlife remains a socialized resource. Not only is this unfortunate for people, but it is counterproductive for wildlife as well.

Countless species have been extirpated from the face of the earth under public ownership and government protection; yet no species of animal that was both privately owned and commercially valued has ever gone extinct. Thus, despite what some environmentalists have argued, putting a price tag on a species does not make it disappear. As long as private rights of use and exclusion are properly defined and adequately enforced, an abundance of diverse wildlife will be supplied if it is demanded through a sufficiently free market. Without secure private property rights, however, commercially valued species are as likely to be extinguished as conserved.

When it comes to conserving wildlife, institutions matter, as do incentives. For wildlife conservation to be successful, the incentives must be either positive or neutral. In the United States, however, those incentives are almost entirely negative. This is especially true under the 1973 U.S. Endangered Species Act (ESA), which penalizes landowners for having endangered species on their property. The penalty for having listed species on your property typically translates into draconian land-use restrictions, extortionate permit requirements, red tape, lost income, lost opportunities, property taxes on land that cannot be used, and cost-prohibitive legal fees. As a result, the ESA has stopped landowners from building homes, constructing roads, plowing fields, felling trees, filling ditches, and even clearing firebreaks to protect their home and family from fire hazards.

These broad constraints on U.S. agriculture have turned many farmers and ranchers against the Endangered Species Act and the species it ostensibly aims to protect. In short, the ESA has produced enemies of wildlife, not defenders of wildlife. It has encouraged habitat destruction, not conservation. As a result, the ESA has failed in its mission to recover threatened and endangered species, and it will continue to fail until Congress fundamentally reforms the law. That is why ESA reform is imperative for rural landowners as well as for the species that currently inhabit their property and those that might in the future.

An Environmental Train Wreck

If one assumes that feeding, clothing, and sheltering human beings constitute legitimate economic pursuits, then one might also assume that government should and will continue to allow private landowners to produce such products. And yet the ESA can be used as a brake on commodity production, as it has been in the past. Thus, the potential for conflict is obvious, as the General Accounting Office discovered in 1994 when it reported that more than 75 percent of all threatened and endangered species in the United States depend on private land for all or some of their habitat needs. Given that the primary use of rural land continues to be agriculture, agriculture is on a collision course with the ESA. Given that some biologists estimate that as many as 250,000 species living in the United States have yet to be identified by science and that they almost surely will be "listed" under the ESA if and when they are identified, the train wreck ahead is clearly visible.

For some, the train has already wrecked.

Andy and Cindy Domenigoni (of western Riverside County, California) fallowed 800 acres of farmland, to rest and rejuvenate their soil, just as the family has done for five generations. When the Interior Department's U.S. Fish and Wildlife Service (FWS) listed the Stephens' kangaroo rat as an endangered subspecies in 1988, the Domenigonis were told they could no longer farm their fields. Their land was "frozen." By fallowing their fields, the Domenigonis had allowed kangaroo rats to take up residence on their land, and for this they were punished. In addition to costing several hundred thousand dollars in lost income and attorneys' fees, the family's 800 acres of rat habitat also provided the bulk of the fuel for a fire that burned down 29 homes on October 27, 1993.

Barnett. © 1997 by Jerry Barnett. Reproduced by permission.

The FWS had prohibited "disking" firebreaks and farming in designated rat habitat, and the Domenigonis had allowed rat habitat to grow by fallowing their fields. As a result, their fields were overgrown with brush and thus became a tinderbox, which fueled the destruction of property owned by close neighbors. After the fire, ironically, the FWS told the Domenigonis they could begin farming again. In fact, the FWS informed the Domenigonis that before the fire their fields had become too overgrown with brush to provide good rat habitat anyway. Thus, because of rat habitat that the FWS later claimed did not exist during much of the time the federal government was regulating it, the family lost approximately $400,000 in farming income, and many of their neighbors lost their homes.

Another egregious example from California involved Tang Ming-Lin, a Taiwanese immigrant who bought 723 acres of undeveloped farmland in Kern County, all of which was zoned for agriculture. One day in 1994, when his fore-man was plowing a new field, some 20 government agents (6 of whom were armed) raided his farm and confiscated his tractor. His crime? Tang Ming-Lin had allowed his foreman to plow land inhabited by endangered species, a federal crime. Specifically, the FWS claimed that Ming-Lin's fore-man had killed two (possibly five) Tipton kangaroo rats and "taken" the habitat of blunt-nosed leopard lizards and San Joaquin kit foxes. The FWS never provided any evidence, but it did demand 363 of Ming-Lin's 723 acres, $300,000 in fines, and $172,425 to maintain the expropriated land as a wildlife preserve.

The FWS raided Ming-Lin's offices and slandered his family in the media. Among other outrages, the FWS threat-ened to deport his family and implicated them in tax fraud and other nefarious schemes, all of which turned out to be untrue. One FWS official even managed to convince local authorities to suspend the immigrant's driver's license. In the end, however, the FWS backed down when faced with a jury trial. Tang Ming-Lin's persecution had sparked a property-rights backlash. Although he admitted to no wrongdoing, Ming-Lin did agree to donate $5,000 to a habitat conserva-tion fund and to stop farming his land until he obtained an ESA permit. This episode awakened people to what the ESA could do to farmers and ranchers.

Fails to Save Endangered Species

As we have seen, the bulk of the ESA's costs and burdens are borne by the unlucky people who own or lease the wrong pieces of land. As Jim Huffman, dean of the Northwestern School of Law at Lewis and Clark College, has written: "The pervasive notion that society can avoid the costs of public action if government can avoid compensating for property affected is simple self-deception. The costs of gov-ernment action will be borne by someone. The compensa-tion requirement, like a rule of liability, simply determines who that someone is."

There is no doubt that the ESA has run roughshod over the lives and liberties of some people, a fact that some envi-ronmentalists still try to deny. Nor is there any doubt that, after 25 years of regulation, the ESA has been a complete and utter failure.

Although the act's statutory objective is to recover listed species, none have recovered due to the ESA. *Not a single one.* As of September 1999, only 27 species (out of more than 1,150 currently on the list) have been removed from the ESA's list of protected species. Seven of those species were "delisted" because they went extinct. Nine of them, according to the FWS, were "data errors," which means they never should have been listed in the first place. The FWS, the Interior Department agency charged with implementing and enforcing the act, only claims to have "recovered" the remaining 11 (of 27) delisted species, but not one of them was saved by the ESA.

Thus, based on the record to date, a species is more likely to go extinct under the ESA than it is to recover (11 extinctions versus 0 recoveries). This is sad but true, much like the reasons for the ESA's abysmal failure.

Reforming the Endangered Species Act

If society wants more of something, it would do well to reward those who provide it, not punish them. Instead, the ESA has turned wildlife assets into regulatory liabilities. People tend to protect assets and eliminate liabilities, which is largely why the ESA has failed so miserably. Solving this problem, however, is easier on paper than it is in practice. It is all but a foregone conclusion that we will be stuck with some sort of federal ESA for the foreseeable future. Thus, if repeal is not a viable option, reform is imperative.

In the absence of punitive regulations, most landowners would gladly host threatened and endangered species on their property. Some would even go out of their way to ensure that rare wildlife had every chance to recover on their land. In many cases, landowners would need no other incentive than the assurance that they will not be regulated for having such species on their property. In other cases, positive incentives might be necessary. With minor clarifications, the ESA's land acquisition provision could provide all the authority needed by the secretary of the interior to pursue all manner of positive inducements. And, of course, there is no law barring private environmental groups from purchasing habitat or easements or otherwise putting their money where their values are.

For many people in the agricultural community and elsewhere, ESA reform is a simple matter of justice. Surely, the cost of satisfying the public's desire to protect publicly owned wildlife would qualify as a public burden that should not be foisted on certain people who happen to own the last remnants of certain habitats.

After all, the people who own that land are those who refrained from modifying endangered species habitat; that is why they still *have* such habitat. While everyone else was busy building homes, office buildings, malls, and restaurants, those landowners were busy growing habitat. Now we have the temerity to tell them that they owe us. We make our demands as we sit in the same homes and office buildings that destroyed previous habitat, oblivious to the fact that the owners of today's habitat are literally, almost by definition, the last people who deserve to be blamed or punished.

Thus, solving this problem of publicly owned wildlife residing on privately owned habitat is the main goal of true ESA reform. The trick is to do it without treating private land as if it were legally owned or controlled by the government.

> *"Fire is inevitable in many forest and grassland habitats. It is an eloquent promoter of diversity."*

Controlled Fires Are Beneficial to Forests

John Stuart

Wildfires in the American Southwest, such as those that swept Southern California in October 2003, can destroy millions of acres of forests and developed land. While uncontrolled wildfires are devastating, many environmentalists assert that fires that are carefully set and controlled by fire departments and forest managers can benefit forests. In the following viewpoint John Stuart contends that the United States should end its fire-suppression policies and reconsider the use of controlled fires. He asserts that prescribed fires help create fertile soil for new trees and promote the germination of diverse plants, many of which help sustain deer and other herbivores. Stuart is a writer for *Mother Earth News*, an environmental magazine.

As you read, consider the following questions:
1. How many acres were burned in the Biscuit Fire, according to Stuart?
2. According to the author, how did forest management practices change during the 1990s?
3. In Stuart's view what will be the likely effects of the two initiatives proposed by President George W. Bush?

In my early years working for a volunteer fire department, the mission could not have been more clear: Control the chaos, save the house, put the fire out!

During the same years, I worked on controlled burns on commercial forests, where we operated under an entirely different understanding. Here, fire was fulfilling its beneficial, primeval mission. Low flames crackled across the hillsides, reducing to ash the incendiary branches and needles that could have fueled large destructive fires some time in the future. After the burns, the enriched soil provided a fertile bed for new tree seedlings. Valuable nutrients in the ash were absorbed quickly by the emerging vegetation.

The Benefits of Fire

Decades of research (and a certain amount of common sense) show that fire is not only beneficial in many natural settings, but that it is necessary to sustain the life cycles of many living things.

Fire is inevitable in many forest and grassland habitats. It is an eloquent promoter of diversity. Walk through a burned area in the years following a fire and watch the amazing parade of emerging life. Mushrooms sprout; fruit-bearing shrubs—roses, vacciniums (blueberries, huckleberries) and the Rubus genus (raspberries, blackberries)—can cover hundreds of acres within five years after a fire. The animals follow. Brushy plants and grasses that sprout after a fire are haute cuisine for the big herbivores: moose, elk and deer.

[In the summer of 2002,] the Biscuit Fire burned a national forest in Oregon. Although the perimeter encompassed 500,000 acres, about half of these acres burned lightly or not at all. Much of the media covered the event as a tragedy for the natural environment. In fact it was just the kind of fire that promotes healthy plant and animal life. Greg Clevenger, a local staff officer for the Rogue River and Siskiyou National Forests, points out that fire "goes in and cleans out a lot of fuel buildup. What people tend to forget is, it will grow back. I'm not saying all fires are good all the time. But we tend as a society to sensationalize and overdramatize the effect. Fire is a natural process. It plays a role like the wind and the rain."

After a series of very destructive fires in the Great Lakes region in the late 1800s and several large fires in the early 1900s, the U.S. Forest Service established a policy to stop all fires in national forests. Fires on private land already were being doused, but this was the first time large-scale fire prevention was attempted on sprawling public lands. Early 20th-century foresters, focusing on the monetary value of trees, viewed all fires as detrimental. Sawmill owners and logging companies did not want their commodities going up in smoke. And national forest decision-makers, who were being trained in the same tradition as private foresters, worked under the same assumptions. Our appreciation for the ecological benefits of fire would be decades in coming.

Paying for Suppressed Fires

The longer vegetation accumulates, the more destructive an eventual fire will be. Years of amassed underbrush lit by lightning or carelessly tended campfires can fuel a much hotter, faster-moving fire than would naturally occur. . . .

These infernos—known as crown fires—consume whole stands of trees at once. Crown fires burn so hot and deep that they destroy the roots of trees. Without roots to anchor the soil, heavy rains erode topsoil and sweep it into rivers. "We're paying for all those decades that Smokey the Bear suppressed fires," says Karl Brown of the U.S. Geological Survey.

Michael Cannell, *Science World*, February 22, 1999.

Before forest managers got involved, frequent, low-intensity fires burned off the brush and small trees (the most flammable stuff) in many ecological environments. The bigger trees survived, and benefited from the regular deposits of nutrient-rich ash. Large trees, widely spaced on the ground, with limbs high in the air, are fairly fire-resistant.

Logging of these big trees has resulted in crowded stands of young trees, much more vulnerable to fire.

As the science of ecology revealed the benefits of fire in many forests, forest management practices changed. In the 1990s, logging levels were decreased, wide protective buffers were established along streams and a general feeling emerged that national forest policy was beginning to value preservation over extraction. Unfortunately, that feeling didn't last.

Wilderness or Commodity

Again today, we face powerful forces that view our national forests as commodities. In late August 2002, President, [George W.] Bush made a strategically timed appearance near the Biscuit Fire in Oregon to promote the National Fire Plan (NFP) and a new program, the Healthy Forests Initiative (HFI). Both the NFP and HFI attempt to increase logging in national forests, using fire as a scare story to promote new plans that will have little to do with fire but that will increase logging dramatically.

Despite the stir raised by the media about the "catastrophe" or "disaster" of wildfires, the 6 to 8 million acres per year burned in several recent years are not extraordinary; between 1919 and 1949, an average of 29 million acres per year burned on all lands, public and private.

The Northwest Forest Plan was designed specifically to protect rare species and their old-growth habitat in the Cascade forests of Washington, Oregon and northern California. The reporting requirements of the Northwest Forest Plan that the HFI criticizes as holding up timber sales were put in place specifically to ensure that things like wildlife habitat, recreation and water quality are considered when logging plans are drafted. The Endangered Species Act, the National Environmental Policy Act and others that govern the preparation of timber sales were enacted by citizens who value conservation of our national forests. The comment and appeal regulations that HFI criticizes have given the American people some real control over what happens on public lands.

The national forests, in fact, are the largest reservoirs of wildlife habitat in this country. Sometimes people need to visit the woods, too, to experience a little of the wilderness—and wildness—themselves.

Increasing development of rural lands surrounding the national forests is steadily reducing their complexity and wildness. Fire is just one of many natural elements, sometimes peaceful, sometimes threatening, that make forests work.

Those in favor of more logging are wordsmithing fire into the latest "catastrophic" force to justify more tree-cutting. Hopefully, the American people will think otherwise.

"Even the best-planned fire can go out of control."

Controlled Fires Are Harmful to Forests

Thomas M. Bonnicksen

In the following viewpoint Thomas M. Bonnicksen argues that popular methods of fire prevention, such as thinning and controlled fires, are ineffective at preventing large, devastating wildfires. According to Bonnicksen, thinning forests will not keep fires small, while prescribed fires are difficult to control and can create massive conflagrations, such as the one that ravaged Yellowstone National Park in 1988. He concludes that the best way to sustain forests is through active management. Bonnicksen is a professor of forest science at Texas A&M University and the author of *America's Ancient Forests: From the Ice Age to the Age of Discovery*.

As you read, consider the following questions:
1. According to the author, why have forests become thicker and more hazardous?
2. In Bonnicksen's opinion why is the Forest Service reluctant to support logging?
3. Why should today's forests be modeled after America's original forests, according to the author?

The devastating fire that swept over Los Alamos, N.M. [in May 2000] is only the symptom of a far more serious problem. We are letting America's native forests deteriorate and burn.

The Los Alamos fire, also known as the Cerro Grande fire, is just one among thousands of fires that ravage Western forests each year, and they are growing worse. So far [in 2000] 81,697 fires burned 6.9 million acres. By comparison, the 10-year average is 64,908 fires burning 2.9 million acres. The average fire size this year is 85 acres, more than double the 10-year average of 44 acres. Suppression costs are about $15 million per day and may reach $1 billion by year-end, and property losses and forest restoration costs could easily cause that total to double.

Fires Have Become More Dangerous

The reason for this problem is simple. Today's forests are a tattered and unhealthy remnant of the original forests. More than a century ago, we began to protect forests from fires, and we set some forests aside in parks and reserves to protect them from humans. We did not consider that our forests had evolved with lightning fires and more than 12,000 years of burning, cutting, and other uses by native peoples. Now, we have succeeded in putting out most of the little fires that kept forests open and clear of debris, and we have nearly shut down timber management on the national forests. Therefore, our forests are growing older, thicker, and more hazardous, and fires can rarely be stopped during hot dry periods.

In the Southwest, ponderosa pine forests (like those that burned at Los Alamos) are 31 times denser than the original forests. So it is not surprising that fires are larger and more destructive, that plant and animal species are disappearing, that streams are drying as thickets of trees use up the water, and that insects and disease are reaching epidemic proportions.

The original forests were open and patchy, but now they are so thick that any fire has the potential for turning a forest into a colossal furnace. That is what happened in Montana's Bitterroot Mountains [in 2000,] where fires destroyed 300,000 acres of forest. Much of it was ponderosa pine, which is a forest that normally burns with small and light fires that do little damage to the larger trees.

Drastic cuts in trained personnel within federal agencies make the fire problem worse. On Jan. 3, 2000, Lester Rosenkrance, Bureau of Land Management (BLM) Director for Fire and Aviation, sent a memo to Director Tom Fry stating, "There is no doubt in my mind that we are placing the public and property at greater risk as our ability to respond quickly and aggressively to wildland fires decreases." He added that, "Should calamity strike, the agencies will be held accountable." The BLM Director ignored Rosenkrance's warning and transferred him to another job.

Thinning Forests Will Not Help

The National Park Service and other federal agencies argue that prescribed fires and thinning will reduce the fire hazard. Thinning, from their point-of-view, means removing "the trees causing the problem." Specifically, it means little trees that grow under big trees. However, it is not just little trees that cause the problem. Historically, our forests were fragmented. They formed a mosaic of patches containing different sizes of trees. This confined the hotter fires to mostly older patches, because patches of younger trees do not burn well.

In some forests, such as ponderosa pine, even the older patches burned light because fires were so frequent. Now that small fires and cutting are no longer creating new openings for young trees, this patchiness is disappearing. Thus, forests have become more uniform, and fires spread over vast areas. Thinning little trees may make an older forest less flammable, but it does nothing to restore the natural mosaic that regenerated young trees and kept fires small. Thinning also does nothing to restore and sustain the diverse array of wildlife and plants that depend on the patchiness of a forest.

Equally important, thinning is expensive. Forest Service managers design timber sales to ease the fire danger, but nobody's buying. The Forest Service is trying to sell just the little trees, and then they want timber companies to use helicopter logging. But who can afford to harvest the least valuable trees with the most expensive logging methods? No wonder nobody is buying.

The Forest Service refuses to use logging as a tool to restore the natural patchiness and diversity of a forest, because that would require allowing the timber companies to remove some big trees. At the same time, the Forest Service is willing to forego the expertise and money these companies would contribute to restoring our forests. Instead, it would rather ask taxpayers to pay hundreds of millions of dollars a year to use non-commercial thinning.

A Threat to Mature Trees

Some experts are convinced that even low-intensity fires— including so-called prescribed fires set to clear out the understory—pose grave dangers to large, mature trees. A quarter-century ago, in fact, [Wally] Covington and two Forest Service researchers experimented with the use of prescribed fire in the Coconino National Forest. Their reasoning seemed sound: since fire exclusion had created the problem, the solution must lie in bringing fire back. Alas, the results were contrary to expectations. The dog-hair thickets of young trees the scientists hoped to kill survived, and the old-growth trees they hoped to save died.

Why? In the absence of fire, too much fuel, in the form of dropped needles and branches, had accumulated at the bases of the largest trees. Yet not enough time had elapsed to allow a similar buildup of fuel beneath the crowns of the smaller trees. As a consequence, flames traveled quickly through the thickets of new growth but smoldered long enough at the feet of the giant trees to girdle and kill them.

J. Madeleine Nash, *Time*, August 18, 2003.

The Forest Service then accepts the unnatural forests that this method creates. U.S. Representative Helen Chenoweth-Hage (R.-Id.), Chairman of the Subcommittee on Forests and Forest Health, summed it up when she said, "The USDA Forest Service has gone from being a model of federal organizational effectiveness to 'the gang that can't shoot straight.'"

Why Prescribed Fires Do Not Work

Prescribed fire creates many of the same problems as thinning, and it is equally expensive. It is also extremely dangerous. Even the best-planned fire can go out of control. The fire set by Bandelier National Monument [near Los Alamos] officials, under conditions that anyone would call extreme, is indefensible.

At Bandelier, they intended to "restore fire as a keystone natural process and to reduce hazard fuels." Instead, they created the Los Alamos fire. They set the fire knowing it was the second year of drought caused by La Niña. They even failed to heed a U.S. Weather Service warning that the potential for fire growth was extreme. It was becoming too dry and windy for a prescribed fire but they lit it anyway. Bandelier superintendent Roy Weaver even told the *Albuquerque Tribune*, "we knew this one was going to be pushing the limits a little bit."

Park staff did the same thing in Yellowstone National Park in 1985, when they let a fire burn until it became impossible to control. When it was over, the fire had charred nearly one-half of our oldest national park. An internal memo documented that the park staff "were determined" to let the fires burn although they knew it "was a very dry year."

Just like park staff at Bandelier, Yellowstone personnel remain unrepentant to this day. They continue to blame "Mother Nature" for high winds and drought. The Los Alamos fire, the let-it-burn Yellowstone fire, and the fires of 2000 are ominous signs of what lies ahead. The forest fire menace is growing more serious each year, and we are not using what we know to prevent it. . . .

Active Management Is the Answer

We have reached a turning point in the history of our forests. Unless we begin a large-scale restoration forestry program now, many of America's native forests will further deteriorate, and some may cease to exist within a few decades. The best way to reverse the decline is to use the original forests as models for future forests. The native forests that European explorers found, provide excellent models for management because of their beauty, diversity, and abundance of wildlife. They also were inherently sustainable.

However, this goal cannot be achieved by "letting nature take-its-course" or with prescribed fire alone. It requires *active management*. We must use the safest and most cost-effective tools available to restore health and diversity to America's forests.

Periodical Bibliography

The following articles have been selected to supplement the diverse views presented in this chapter.

Lester Brown	"Reframing the Big Picture," *Hope*, September/October 2003.
Michael Cannell	"Fighting Fire with Fire," *Science World*, February 22, 1999.
Ken Conca	"American Environmentalism Confronts the Global Economy," *Dissent*, Winter 2000.
Mary H. Cooper	"Setting Environmental Priorities," *CQ Researcher*, May 21, 1999.
Michael De Alessi	"Entrepreneurs and the Environment," *World & I*, April 2001.
William Greider	"The Greening of American Capitalism," *OnEarth*, Fall 2003.
Sam Hitt	"A Duty to Conserve," *Wild Earth*, Spring 2002.
Dwight R. Lee	"Getting the Most Out of Pollution," *Ideas on Liberty*, October 2001.
Tibor R. Machan	"Radical Free Market Environmentalism," *Free Inquiry*, Summer 2001.
J. Madeleine Nash	"Fireproofing the Forests," *Time*, August 18, 2003.
Robert R. Nelson	"Western Myths and Realities," *Regulation*, Summer 2002.
Danielle Nierenberg	"U.S. Environmental Policy: Where Is It Headed?" *World Watch*, July/August 2001.
Kenneth J. Ruffing	"Achieving Sustainability," *Forum for Applied Research and Public Policy*, Winter 1999.
Ron Steffens	"What Is a WFU (and Why Should a Conservationist Care)?" *Wild Earth*, Fall 1999.
David Zink	"Profit Pollution and Socialist Solutions," *Political Affairs*, May 2003.

For Further Discussion

Chapter 1

1. After reading the viewpoints in this chapter, what do you think is the most serious environmental problem addressed by the authors? What, if any, environmental issues do you consider to be more troubling? Explain your answers.

2. Global warming is a controversial topic throughout the scientific community. After reading the articles by George M. Woodwell and John F. McManus, do you think scientists will be able to reach an agreement on whether global warming is a problem? In addition, which writer do you believe uses scientific data more effectively? Explain your answers.

3. John Attarian asserts that both sides of the population debate have misinterpreted Thomas Malthus. What specific criticisms do you think Attarian would have of Stephen Moore's viewpoint? Would you agree with his criticisms? Why or why not?

Chapter 2

1. The Sierra Club and Steve Seachman disagree on the success of the Clean Water Act. Do you believe that federal government regulations are the best method of reducing water pollution, or should individual cities and states have more control over their pollution-control policies? Explain your answers.

2. If you agree with John R.E. Bliese's contention that renewable energy can reduce pollution, what steps would you take to make such energy sources more affordable? If, on the other hand, you agree with Jerry Taylor's criticism of renewable energy, what do you think are the most compelling arguments against its use? Explain your answers.

3. After reading the viewpoints by Sam Martin and Daniel Benjamin, do you support mandatory recycling programs? Why or why not?

Chapter 3

1. After reading the viewpoints in this chapter, do you believe that your lifestyle is harmful to the environment? If so, what steps would you take to reduce your ecological impact? Explain your answers.

2. The original title of Albert Koehl's viewpoint is "A Modest Proposal," which was also the title of a famous piece of satire by the seventeenth-century writer Jonathan Swift. Do you believe that Koehl's satirical defense of sport utility vehicle (SUV) drivers is

an effective way for him to express his criticisms of SUVs, or do you feel that his message is bogged down by sarcasm? Explain your response.

3. Jutka Terris and Jane S. Shaw disagree on the effects suburban sprawl has on wildlife. Which author do you believe offers a more compelling argument and why? Furthermore, given that suburban sprawl is an unalterable reality, what steps, if any, would you take to ensure that humans and animals can coexist in the same habitats?

Chapter 4

1. Several of the viewpoints in this chapter consider the effectiveness of environmental policies that rely on free-market economics. After reading the chapter, do you believe the free-market approach can improve the environment? Explain your answer.

2. John D. Dingell and Ike C. Sugg use statistics to bolster their opposing views on the Endangered Species Act. Whose use of statistics do you find more convincing and why?

3. John Stuart asserts that fires can benefit forests by spurring the germination of new plants and creating fertile soil for trees. He recommends using prescribed fires to achieve those results, but simply allowing naturally occurring fires to burn would accomplish the same goals. Do you believe there are times when people should allow nature to run its course? For example, should state and federal governments let some naturally occurring fires burn? Similarly, should people permit natural predator/prey relationships to determine species' populations rather than rely on hunting? Explain your answers, drawing from this chapter or other relevant sources. Use any examples you wish of situations where people intervene to control nature for the benefit of the environment.

Organizations to Contact

The editors have compiled the following list of organizations concerned with the issues debated in this book. The descriptions are derived from materials provided by the organizations. All have publications or information available for interested readers. The list was compiled on the date of publication of the present volume; the information provided here may change. Be aware that many organizations take several weeks or longer to respond to inquiries, so allow as much time as possible.

American Council on Science and Health (ACSH)
1995 Broadway, 2nd Floor, New York, NY 10023-5860
(212) 362-7044 • fax: (212) 362-4919
e-mail: acsh@acsh.org • Web site: www.acsh.org
ACSH is a consumer education consortium concerned with environmental and health-related issues. The council publishes the quarterly *Priorities*, position papers such as "Global Climate Change and Human Health," and numerous reports, including *Arsenic, Drinking Water, and Health* and *The DDT Ban Turns 30*.

Canadian Centre for Pollution Prevention (C2P2)
100 Charlotte St., Sarnia, ON N7T 4R2 Canada
(800) 667-9790 • fax: (519) 337-3486
e-mail: info@c2p2online.com • Web site: www.c2p2online.com
The Canadian Centre for Pollution Prevention is Canada's leading resource on ways to end pollution. It provides access to national and international information on pollution and prevention, online forums, and publications, including *Practical Pollution Training Guide* and the newsletter *at the source*, which C2P2 publishes three times a year.

Cato Institute
1000 Massachusetts Ave. NW, Washington, DC 20001-5403
(202) 842-0200 • fax: (202) 842-3490
e-mail: cato@cato.org • Web site: www.cato.org
The Cato Institute is a libertarian public policy research foundation that aims to limit the role of government and protect civil liberties. The institute believes EPA regulations are too stringent. Publications offered on the Web site include the bimonthly *Cato Policy Report*, the quarterly journal *Regulation*, the paper "The EPA's Clear Air-ogance," and the book *Climate of Fear: Why We Shouldn't Worry About Global Warming*.

Competitive Enterprise Institute (CEI)
1001 Connecticut Ave. NW, Suite 1250, Washington, DC 20036
(202) 331-1010 • fax: (202) 331-0640
e-mail: info@cei.org • Web site: www.cei.org

CEI is a nonprofit public policy organization dedicated to the principles of free enterprise and limited government. The institute believes private incentives and property rights, rather than government regulations, are the best way to protect the environment. CEI's publications include the newsletter *Monthly Planet* (formerly *CEI Update*), *On Point* policy briefs, and the books *Global Warming and Other Eco-Myths* and *The True State of the Planet.*

Environmental Protection Agency (EPA)
Ariel Rios Building
1200 Pennsylvania Ave. NW, Washington, DC 20460
(202) 272-0167
Web site: www.epa.gov

The EPA is the federal agency in charge of protecting the environment and controlling pollution. The agency works toward these goals by enacting and enforcing regulations, identifying and fining polluters, assisting businesses and local environmental agencies, and cleaning up polluted sites. The EPA publishes periodic reports and the monthly *EPA Activities Update.*

Environment Canada
351 St. Joseph Blvd., Gatineau, QC K1A 0H3 Canada
(819) 997-2800 • (800) 668-6767
fax: (819) 953-2225 • TTY: (819) 994-0736
e-mail: enviroinfo@ec.gc.ca • Web site: www.ec.gc.ca

Environment Canada is a department of the Canadian government. Its goal is the achievement of sustainable development in Canada through conservation and environmental protection. The department publishes reports, including *Environmental Signals 2003*, and fact sheets on a number of topics, such as acid rain and pollution prevention.

Foundation for Clean Air Progress (FCAP)
1801 K St. NW, Suite 1000L, Washington, DC 20036
(800) 272-1604
e-mail: info@cleanairprogress.org
Web site: www.cleanairprogress.org

FCAP is a nonprofit organization that believes the public is unaware of the progress that has been made in reducing air pollution. The foundation represents various sectors of business and industry in providing information to the public about improving air quality trends. FCAP publishes reports and studies demonstrating that air pollution is on the decline, including *Breathing Easier About Energy—a Healthy Economy and Healthier Air* and *Study on Air Quality Trends, 1970–2015.*

Global Warming International Center (GWIC)
22W381 75th St., Naperville, IL 60565
(630) 910-1551 • fax: (630) 910-1561
Web site: www.globalwarming.net

GWIC is an international body that provides information on global warming science and policy to industries and governmental and nongovernmental organizations. The center sponsors research supporting the understanding of global warming and ways to reduce the problem. It publishes the quarterly newsletter *World Resource Review.*

National Resources Defense Council (NRDC)
40 W. 20th St., New York, NY 10011
(212) 727-2700 • fax: (212) 727-1773
e-mail: nrdcinfo@nrdc.org • Web site: www.nrdc.org

The NRDC is a nonprofit organization with more than four hundred thousand members. It uses laws and science to protect the environment, including wildlife and wild places. NRDC publishes the quarterly magazine *OnEarth* (formerly *Amicus Journal*) and hundreds of reports, including *Development and Dollars* and the annual report *Testing the Waters.*

Pew Center on Global Climate Change
2101 Wilson Blvd., Suite 550, Arlington, VA 22201
(703) 516-4146 • fax: (703) 841-1422
Web site: www.pewclimate.org

The Pew Center is a nonpartisan organization dedicated to educating the public and policy makers about the causes and potential consequences of global climate change and informing them of ways to reduce the emissions of greenhouse gases. Its reports include *Designing a Climate-Friendly Energy Policy* and *The Science of Climate Change.*

Political Economy Research Center (PERC)
2048 Analysis Dr., Suite A, Bozeman, MT 59718
(406) 587-9591
e-mail: perc@perc.org • Web site: www.perc.org

PERC is a nonprofit research and educational organization that seeks market-oriented solutions to environmental problems. The center holds a variety of conferences and provides environmental educational material. It publishes the quarterly newsletter *PERC Reports*, commentaries, research studies, and policy papers, among them *Economic Growth and the State of Humanity* and *The National Forests: For Whom and for What?*

Sierra Club
85 Second St., Second Floor, San Francisco, CA 94105-3441
(415) 977-5500 • fax: (415) 977-5799
e-mail: information@sierraclub.org • Web site: www.sierraclub.org

The Sierra Club is a grassroots organization with chapters in every state that promotes the protection and conservation of natural resources. The organization maintains separate committees on air quality, global environment, and solid waste, among other environmental concerns, to help achieve its goals. It publishes books, fact sheets, the bimonthly magazine *Sierra* and the *Planet* newsletter, which appears several times a year.

Union of Concerned Scientists (UCS)
2 Brattle Square, Cambridge, MA 02238
(617) 547-5552 • fax: (617) 864-9405
e-mail: ucs@ucsusa.org • Web site: www.ucsusa.org

UCS aims to advance responsible public policy in areas where science and technology play important roles. Its programs emphasize transportation reform, arms control, safe and renewable energy technologies, and sustainable agriculture. UCS publications include the twice-yearly magazine *Catalyst*, the quarterly newsletter *earthwise*, and the reports *Greener SUVs* and *Greenhouse Crisis: The American Response*.

Worldwatch Institute
1776 Massachusetts Ave. NW, Washington, DC 20036-1904
(202) 452-1999 • fax: (202) 296-7365
e-mail: worldwatch@worldwatch.org
Web site: www.worldwatch.org

Worldwatch is a nonprofit public policy research organization dedicated to informing the public and policy makers about emerging global problems and trends and the complex links between the environment and the world economy. Its publications include *Vital Signs*, issued every year, the bimonthly magazine *World Watch*, the Environmental Alert series, and numerous policy papers, including "Unnatural Disasters" and "City Limits: Putting the Brakes on Sprawl."

Bibliography of Books

Ronald Bailey, ed.   *Earth Report 2000: Revisiting the True State of the Planet.* New York: McGraw-Hill, 2000.

John J. Berger   *Beating the Heat: Why and How We Must Combat Global Warming.* Berkeley, CA: Berkeley Hills Books, 2000.

John R.E. Bliese   *The Greening of Conservative America.* Boulder, CO: Westview Press, 2001.

Daniel Botkin et al.   *Forces of Change: A New View of Nature.* Washington, DC: National Geographic Society, 2000.

Michael Brower and Warren Leon   *The Consumer's Guide to Effective Environmental Choices: Practical Advice from the Union of Concerned Scientists.* New York: Three Rivers Press, 1999.

Pamela S. Chasek, ed.   *The Global Environment in the Twenty-First Century: Prospects for International Cooperation.* Tokyo: United Nations University Press, 2000.

Jack Doyle   *Taken for a Ride: Detroit's Big Three and the Politics of Pollution.* New York: Four Walls Eight Windows, 2000.

Simon Dresner   *The Principles of Sustainability.* London: Earthscan, 2002.

Richard Ellis   *The Empty Ocean: Plundering the World's Marine Life.* Washington, DC: Island Press/Shearwater Books, 2003.

Hilary French   *Vanishing Borders: Protecting the Planet in the Age of Globalization.* New York: W.W. Norton, 2000.

Ron Fridell   *Global Warming.* New York: Franklin Watts, 2002.

Michael H. Glantz   *Climate Affairs: A Primer.* Washington, DC: Island Press, 2003.

Indur Goklany   *Clearing the Air: The Real Story of the War on Air Pollution.* Washington, DC: Cato Institute, 1999.

Joyeeta Gupta   *Our Simmering Planet: What to Do About Global Warming?* London: Zed Books, 2001.

Peter W. Huber   *Hard Green: Saving the Environment from the Environmentalists: A Conservative Manifesto.* New York: Basic Books, 1999.

Robert Hunter   *Thermageddon: Countdown to 2030.* New York: Arcade, 2003.

Klaus M. Leisinger, Karen Schmitt, and Rajul Pandya-Lorch
: *Six Billion and Counting: Population Growth and Food Security in the 21st Century.* Washington, DC: International Food Policy Research Institute, 2002.

Bjøasrn Lomborg
: *The Skeptical Environmentalist: Measuring the Real State of the World.* Cambridge, UK: Cambridge University Press, 2001.

William McDonough and Michael Braungart
: *Cradle to Cradle: Remaking the Way We Make Things.* New York: North Point Press, 2002.

Patrick J. Michaels and Robert C. Balling Jr.
: *The Satanic Gases: Clearing the Air About Global Warming.* Washington, DC: Cato Institute, 2000.

Edward Moran, ed.
: *The Global Ecology.* New York: H.W. Wilson, 1999.

Shannon C. Petersen
: *Acting for Endangered Species: The Statutory Ark.* Lawrence: University Press of Kansas, 2002.

Richard C. Porter
: *The Economics of Waste.* Washington, DC: Resources for the Future, 2002.

Kent E. Portney
: *Taking Sustainable Cities Seriously: Economic Development, the Environment, and Quality of Life in American Cities.* Cambridge, MA: MIT Press, 2003.

Richard P. Reading and Brian Miller, eds.
: *Endangered Animals: A Reference Guide to Conflicting Issues.* Westport, CT: Greenwood Press, 2000.

Philip Shabecoff
: *Earth Rising: American Environmentalism in the 21st Century.* Washington, DC: Island Press, 2000.

Vandana Shiva
: *Water Wars: Privatization, Pollution and Profit.* Cambridge, MA: South End Press, 2002.

Lawrence Slobodkin
: *A Citizen's Guide to Ecology.* Oxford, UK: Oxford University Press, 2003.

Eric R.A.N. Smith
: *Energy, the Environment, and Public Opinion.* Lanham, MD: Rowman & Littlefield, 2002.

Barbara Taylor
: *How to Save the Planet.* New York: Franklin Watts, 2001.

Adam S. Weinberg, David N. Pellow, and Allan Schnailberg
: *Urban Recycling and the Search for Sustainable Development.* Princeton, NJ: Princeton University Press, 2000.

Edward O. Wilson
: *The Future of Life.* New York: Alfred A. Knopf, 2002.

Colin Woodard
: *Ocean's End: Travels Through Endangered Seas.* New York: Basic Books, 2000.

Index

acid rain, benefits of SO₂ emissions
trading on, 159–60
Adler, Jonathan, 16
*Agenda 21: The Earth Summit Strategy
to Save the Planet* (United Nations),
52, 124–25
agriculture
biogenetically engineered, 127
dependence of, on petroleum, 60
effects of global warming on, 22–24
as pollution source, 117–18
suburban sprawl is not a threat to,
149
air pollution
from food cultivation/processing,
121
has fallen, 136
from plastics production, 104
Albuquerque Tribune (newspaper), 188
Alcorn, Walter, 165
Almasi, David W., 14
aquifers, depletion of, 25, 61–62
societal effects of, 26
asthma, 14
Atlantic Monthly (magazine), 147
Attarian, John, 53
Audubon (magazine), 148
automobiles, 74–75
fuel cell technology and, 94–95
land use required by, 131
U.S. oil consumption and, 136

Balling, Robert, 46, 47
Barliant, Claire, 163
Bartels, Carlton, 160, 161–62, 165
Bayon, Ricardo, 157
beach closings
prevalence of, 83
by sewage discharge, 84–86
Benjamin, Daniel, 108, 155
Bernstam, Mikhail, 70
biomass, is a good electricity-
generating technology, 93
con, 98–99
birth rate, decline in, 69
Bliese, John R.E., 89, 117
Bonnicksen, Thomas M., 184
Brower, Michael, 74, 103
Brown, Lester, 20, 51
Buffett, Warren, 68
Burger, Mike, 163
Bush, George H.W., 15, 158, 168
forest initiatives of, 183
Bush administration, 38
changes to Clean Air Act proposed

by, 77
proposal for military exemptions to
Endangered Species Act, 169–71
"Buy Nothing Day," 124

California gnatcatcher, 140
Cannell, Michael, 182
carbon dioxide (CO₂)
automobile emissions of, 74
North America sinks more than it
emits, 31
rise in atmospheric levels of, 37
is caused by solar activity, 46
will not cause global warming, 50
see also emissions trading
Carter, Jimmy, 15
Cato Institute, 63
Center for Progressive Regulation, 14,
15
Centrone, Michael J., 16
Cerro Grande fire. *See* Los Alamos
fire
Chenoweth-Hage, Helen, 187
Chicago Tribune (newspaper), 66
China
aquifer depletion in, 61
effects of central planning in, 71
one-child policy in, 65, 66–67
Christy, John R., 45, 46
Claybrook, Joan, 134
Clean Air Act (1990 Amendments),
158–59
Clean Water Act (1972), 76
is fraudulent, 85
sewage problem and, 86–87
successes of, 77
Great Lakes, 80–81
Licking River, 79–80
Narragansett Bay, 78–79
climate change, 40–42
see also global warming
Clinton, Bill, 15
Clinton administration, 38, 65
Clowes, Brian, 65
Club of Rome, 64
Cole, Luke, 165, 167
Commission for Racial Justice, 15
Competitive Enterprise Institute, 123
Condorcet, marquis de, 55–56, 60
consumption patterns, of developed
world, destroy the environment,
119–22
con, 123–28
Cooper, Mary H., 18
coral reefs, 18–19